Big Lads and Handbags

Neil Sarin

To Brenda
Best Wishes
Neil

DEDICATION

This book is dedicated to my wife, Donna, and kids. For putting up with all the late nights and missed weekends, all my black eyes, cuts and bruises, and for living with the scars.

CONTENTS

ACKNOWLEDGMENTS

To all the door supervisors I have stood alongside, fought alongside, and laughed alongside. Too many to mention individually, but if you are reading this, you know who you are.

Clyde Harrison, for the brilliant cover photography.

And Finally; all the pissheads, dickheads and arseholes I have came across in my years on the doors. Without you I wouldn't be needed out there, and I wouldn't have my tales to tell.

Foreword.

When you get your badge this does not mean you are a fully fledged, able to deal with anything doorman/woman. It's like passing your driving test. It doesn't mean you're an expert, just that you have done enough to be allowed on the roads. The real learning starts there. Don't expect to be inundated with work. Like any industry you need to network, continue learning and most importantly be willing to do any and all jobs that come along. Take any shift you can, do it well and maybe you will be asked back to do more.

Very few DS have this as their full time job. Most have another source of income to supplement it. DO NOT rely on this job, it can be taken from you in an instant. You can have your license revoked at any time, get arrested or badly hurt. It is not like Roadhouse the movie (I thought you'd be bigger).

Not all people who get a badge are suited to the work. The role is far more complex than people give it credit for. We all started somewhere and were newbie's, but it's important to realise that sometimes this job puts you in difficult circumstances. If you are not up to the challenge you could make a bad situation worse, or get yourself or someone else hurt.

If you still think this job is for you then here are some tips. Contact all companies in your area personally, do not get someone to do it on your behalf. Take any work offered and do the shift. Shut up and learn. Maybe you will get asked back. Take a walk through your town early on a weekend and chat to the DS. Don't turn up pissed. Don't big yourself up and don't turn up when it's busy as they will not welcome you trying to ask lots of questions.

Make sure your appearance is smart. It is more important than you think. Don't be late or cancel shifts at the last minute, because when you become unreliable, you become unemployable. If you find a good boss, stick with them, loyalty is usually rewarded. Get yourself a good pair of boots.

Just to finish off, please don't act the hard man, no one will be impressed and you will just come across as a dick, and never ever stand in a club queue waving your badge expecting to get in for free. They give them out like smarties these days, so again, if I don't know you personally; you will just look like a dick.

Matt Stait.
Doorman, Martial Arts/Self Defence Instructor, Security Industry Trainer.

Then, Now, Why and How.

George Orwell said: "People sleep peaceably in their beds at night only because rough men stand ready to do violence on their behalf."

Neil Sarin said: "People drink peaceably in our venues at night only because rough men stand ready to do violence on their behalf."

We are those men.
Bouncer, doorman, door supervisor....over the years our title has changed, but the job has remained largely the same. I accept there are many competent female door supervisors out there, but for the purpose of the book I shall refer to us all as door supervisors, doormen or door staff.
Being a doorman these days is different to how it was years ago; mind you, there is still a place for your old school doormen, as a lot of punters these days just take the piss out of the newer, younger door supervisors. I agree you still need your talkers on the door, but you need your fighters just as much.
The governing bodies of today are trying to make the modern doorman a peaceful; smiling, non aggressive doorman, who can diffuse any situation verbally adopting a

non aggressive stance, without having to resort to violence or inflicting pain on offending customers. Unfortunately this model doesn't work with the vast majority of customers you will come across, and a lot of training providers don't explain this to some of the deluded candidates attending door courses. These people get their license and go out on the job; then freeze and get punched in the face when the nasty drunk customer doesn't respond to their calming words, and open handed gestures, like they did on his training course....they are supposed to do as they are asked and quietly walk away....at worst shouting nasty things as they go!

People these days think a door supervisors hands are tied with regards to using violence; at the front door, arsehole punters create this imaginary line, that they tell us that we cannot cross, and they even wave their hand back and forwards over the pavement to emphasize this line we cannot cross....I have never seen this line outside of any venue, nor been taught about its existence!

Anyway; they believe the law is fully on their side, and they will stand and call you offensive names (I normally get baldy, egg head, fatty, and fat cunt quite a bit), and then laugh smugly as they tell you that you can't touch them, as that's "assault".....and they will always do this from about eight to ten feet away from you, so you cannot cross "that" line. I must admit though, I am guilty of sometimes grabbing them and dragging them back over "that" line....taking my chances with when they go to the police. To be fair the police in our city centre normally just move them on when they go crying to them about the nasty doormen.

Back in the day we were mainly there to keep the peace via violence; or threat of violence, these days we have to be a practitioner of customer service, meeting and greeting people, having a good local knowledge to be able to give strangers to the city directions to various venues and hotels etc.

We are expected to utilize conflict management skills to diffuse any situations that may arise; I teach conflict management, and I agree to an extent that it has its place in the job....however some people will never respond to conflict management and reasoning, all they respond to is violence, and the more you try to reason with some people the weaker they will think you are, until the point comes where they will try to take you out....sometimes the only way to stop some people is a good hard fucking punch on the chin....because in this day and age all some people understand is violence.

The training course material; in my opinion, does not reflect the reality of the job, once you have passed your course and get a start on a door somewhere, then you start learning.....we say to new starters "watch and listen to the experienced guys you are working with, learn from them, take their techniques and methods and make them your own....make them work for you"

There are some license holders who are deluded about door work; many who got their license via the Olympics, who use their door supervisor license to do static security work or retail security work, feel they can go from that environment and step straight into a nightclub environment....granted some probably can, but the vast majority cannot, and it is at times embarrassing when you advertise for door supervisors and some of these people walk through the door.

They feel that their license creates some form of shield; and that they won't get hurt, or that the rest of the team will be there for the fighting, as they are the new boy and will be allowed to step back and observe when it kicks off.

It's the opposite way round; your badge makes you a target, and you will get hurt if you cannot fight, and you cannot step back and observe when it kicks off, because if you do, your name will become shit in the industry where you work and you will likely not work again.

Anybody considering working on the doors needs to take a

good look at themselves and ask themselves; have I got what it takes?.....am I prepared to run into a bunch of guys fighting, maybe on my own or with one other colleague....to break that fight up and maybe have them turn on me (happened to me...in the quilted camel)....am I prepared to stand my ground with somebody possibly twice my size, and tell him he can't come in, or that he has to leave....am I going to stand by my mates when challenging, or challenged by aggressive groups of people, probably outnumbered?

Am I strong enough?....can I restrain somebody to stop them fighting or to physically eject them from a premises?....hopefully you can at least hold them until a colleague arrives, because if you can't, there's a good chance they will throw you off and turn on you!

Ask yourself all of these things, as these are the day to day realities of door work, not the staged scenarios you see on the governing body approved PowerPoint presentation on your training course, or what you experienced in your conflict management training with a guy who has done one or two nights on the door....and who didn't shout or swear in case he upset anybody.

This is real life.....and if you don't or can't do the job properly....You will get hurt....badly fucking hurt.

There are no training courses which will train you to be the complete doorman; this has to be done on the job. You can attend conflict management courses and train at your local gym; but these are all controlled environments....on the door, and on the nightclub dance floor there are no rules, it is unpredictable, and there is no substitute for hours on the job and getting your hands dirty.

Of course the first course of action should be to try and diffuse the situation; after all, we don't get paid based on how many fights we have each night.

Diffuse it if you can; let them walk away, but if that's not possible then learn to read the signs....action beats reaction....be pro active with a pre emptive strike....be first, be fast, and make the fucker count….make sure they don't want to come back for more!

I could recount loads of tales where I have talked customers down; diffused situations verbally and avoided violent confrontation by optimizing conflict management techniques…..but who wants to read about that?

Do I like being a doorman?....most definitely; do I like violence?.....no I don't, however it is a necessary evil of the job....just like a joiner will at some point hit his thumb with a hammer....a doorman will at some point hit a customer, it is a means to an end, a way to get the job done when conflict resolution has failed.

Over time you become desensitized to the violence; it becomes the norm, it doesn't shock you anymore. I have seen customers scream with fear, faint or vomit because they aren't accustomed to violence, yet the seasoned doorman can witness or partake in violence and not bat an eyelid. Is this a good thing?...yes and no....yes because there will be no hesitation should they have to use violence to resolve a situation, and no because the violence becomes too easy a solution....too readily available, and the more desensitized you become, the more extreme the violence which is deemed acceptable.

Nietzsche said: "Whoever fights monsters should see to it that in the process he does not become a monster."

Back in the day I did it for the money; I was a young apprentice plasterer earning twenty four pounds fifty a week on a government scheme, but could earn twenty pounds a night on the doors for a few hours work....it's not the case now....the average wage out there on doors now is around ten pound an hour, which you then have to pay tax etc on....so some guys working in nightclubs, from maybe eleven o clock until three in the morning are making less than forty quid!

These days I do it for the buzz.....that feeling I get when

the adrenaline kicks in and you know it's going to go off....I don't feel it as much on a shout as I am too busy running and looking where the incident is....but when I'm standing talking to some dickhead, or next to another member of the team and something's building up....I love it, it's like a drug.

It's a mixture of excitement and fear; anyone in this game that tells you they don't get scared is a liar, it's the body's natural biological reaction to be scared, that's the adrenaline release to preparing you for fighting or fucking off (fight or flight).....Or freeze in the case of some doormen!

The trick is to harness that fear and adrenaline release and make it work for you; it makes you faster and stronger, more alert, gives you the advantage over your opponent....but remember he is feeling it too. Ideally you would be striking first if the situation had resorted to violence; as action beats reaction, however if your opponent has caught you off guard and you are having to react to an attack, then you need to do it fast. You need to overcome the freeze that occurs; you need to train yourself to react immediately and strike or fight back without delay, even if your reaction is just to shield or cover up. Your body will also release adrenaline during a physical confrontation to protect you from pain; many a time I have examined myself after a fight and noticed numerous unexplained cuts and bruises, even when I had my earlobe bitten off in a fight, I didn't feel it because of the adrenaline. It's only a few hours later; or the next day that you start to feel the pain from all your lumps and bumps.

After the confrontation the adrenaline will remain in your system until it is absorbed; it has nowhere else to go! You will notice many door staff "hyped up" after a fight, you may also find you have trouble winding down or sleeping if you have had a night with many confrontations, especially if you have had a particularly violent one. You will replay the event in your mind; what if I did this?....what if I did that?.....if you were injured you will ask yourself what could I have done to prevent it, you will try to piece together the series of events in order to make sense of them, Often the more violent the confrontation; and the more severe any injuries which are sustained, then the longer the period of reflection may last for. You may find yourself feeling a little more frisky than normal (your partner will see this as either a good or bad side affect of adrenaline!)

It doesn't normally take me long to get home from working in the town centre; so I will sit and have a cup of tea or something when I get in, give me a chance to wind down a little before I go to bed. If I've had a bad night I will often get some food on the way home and drive down to the sea front; and I'll just sit in the car for a bit with my supper, having my own little debrief in my head.

Different people react and handle things differently; this is just how I do it, through time and experience you will find whichever way suits you best.

I could do a whole chapter on adrenaline; but there are many books etc out there on both this subject; and the subject of the martial arts / real violence crossover by guys much more qualified and well versed than I am; guys like Rory Miller, Geoff Thompson, Marc MacYoung, Lee Morrison and Richard Dimitri....look at their stuff and take from it what you will.

Henry David Thoreau said: "Read the best books first, or you may not have a chance to read them at all."

Back in the early days I would fight for fun; just steam in and hit everybody involved and then drag them out the doors....banging their heads on door handles etc on the way. As I got older and got more interested in the psychology of violence and behaviour; I became more verbal, more practiced at restraining people and trying to diffuse the situation verbally, I also however focused more on striking (for when the talking wasn't working) and pre emptive strikes.

When I'm in a confrontation I'm always aware of my stance; I will be trying to not present a decent target to the other person, my left hand will be up around chest height forming a barrier, left foot forward, and right hand down by my side....right arm slightly bent. The second I get any indication it's going to kick off; whether it be a drop of their shoulder, a step forward, or even a grimace....the right hand comes up to strike the head....with enough force to shake their brain and stop them striking me, ideally it will be on the jaw line, somewhere between the chin and the ear.

This may sound brutal; but I'm not there to be hit, and I would rather they were lying on the ground than I was. Don't get me wrong; once they were neutralized I would still administer any first aid that was necessary, and I always put them in the recovery position until they come round....

Always be aware of your surroundings. When I am working in a club I prefer to stand away from groups of guys, so I can observe them; if I get any indications from their body language or facial expressions (because you can't hear them in a club), that it's getting a bit naughty then I'll go and stand closer....I'll try and listen to what's being said, if I still can't hear then I'll practically stand right next to them, and ask if everything's ok?....nine times out of ten they will disperse, or one of the more placid ones will tell you who was gonna kick off....then you can do whatever you have to do to stop the situation escalating.

Always be aware of yourself as well; how you stand, where you stand, again if it's in a club, try and find a good vantage point where you can see the areas you are covering, but also so you can see your colleagues and vice versa. Personally I prefer to adopt the "thinkers stance"; whereby my right arm is across my chest, and my left arm is bent with my left hand on my chin....from here I normally subconsciously stroke my chin or my top lip with my first finger. It's a classic non aggressive stance; but from there I can shield my face or head from a strike if need be, I can throw a short left hand punch, I can push out with both hands, or I can prevent somebody coming from being and getting a choke on....for me it is the ideal stance, I can react, defend, or counter attack from it, and it is the one I emphasize the most on my training courses.

Musashi said: "A great fighter makes his everyday stance his fighting stance, and his fighting stance his everyday stance."

One thing I detest is doormen standing with their hands in their pockets; it looks lazy, and if they are in your pockets then you can't use them to defend yourself with....also mobile phones....if you are looking down at your phone, texting or whatever, then you aren't aware of what is going on around you..

Any doorman who doesn't have any scars, or has never been in a fight is either very lucky, or is always the last one there. These guys can normally be found keeping bystanders company, or hiding in the toilet while you are fighting. I know one guy who used to always run for the police radio whenever a fight kicked off, and he was the head doorman!

Licensing has ruined the standards of door staff now, before licensing you only worked the door if someone recommended you, now you only have to do a short course to be able to apply for your license, and you can be a doorman.

Some of the bigger suppliers of door staff will start

anybody; they don't care if you are only six stone and can't defend yourself and your mates, they aren't the ones having to rely on you if it kicks off....to them you are simply a means to an end....a way to fill a gap in a Rota and for them make five or six pounds an hour from you. I have seen door staff turn kids like that away when they turn up for shifts.

In my opinion licensing has done less for the industry as opposed to more.

I deliver the training courses to become a door supervisor; and have taught people who I would never stand shoulder to shoulder with, but if they pass their exams then they pass the course. We try to inject as much realism as possible into the courses, but we have to follow the syllabus as stipulated by the governing body.

A lot of the candidates think that because they have completed their course, that they can do the job, some of these people have never been in any kind of conflict; have never hit or been hit, are offended by foul language, have no physical strength or idea of body mechanics. Not much good when somebody full of drink and drugs is shouting what a fucking arsehole you are while punching your face in!

I obtained my training qualification back in 2011, I attended the five day course to renew my license, and the trainer asked if I had ever considered teaching. From there I went on to obtain my PTLLS (preparing to teach in the lifelong learning sector), delivery of conflict management training, delivery of physical intervention training, and first aid instructor qualifications.

When I deliver the training to door supervisors, I try to prepare them as much as I can for the realities of the job, not only for their benefit, but for the benefit of the guys and girls they are going to go out there and stand alongside; I need to be sure they can all keep themselves and each other safe, we do deliver a bit of conflict management training, which we try to make as realistic as possible, and some physical intervention training.

The physical intervention training has evolved from the health care industry, and uses very soft, non pain compliant techniques. To be fair they would be effective with a compliant, very drunk individual, but totally useless if it all kicks off against someone who is full of drink (and / or drugs) and wants to punch your fucking face in. There are a number of different Physical Intervention systems out there at the minute; some better than others, however it all goes a bit wrong when you try to physically eject someone using one technique, and your colleague tries to eject them using another....it all becomes a bit of a messy clusterfuck. We then go back to learning on the job, watching each other and learning how to work as a team.

A lot of training providers couldn't give a shit, it is just a means to make money for them. They will go through the motions of the course and then spit people out at the end. I have seen new guys on the door with no idea of how to read body language, or how to work as part of a team when diffusing situations or removing people.

A major reason for inadequate training is the trainers themselves. A lot of them have never worked the doors before. To be able to train people you need your basic teaching qualification, and experience in the subject you are teaching (sector competence). This could be from years ago and is easily fabricated, I know one trainer who was delivering cctv training, yet he had never done a cctv course himself and couldn't operate cctv; but his pal had a cctv business and said he had worked there!

That's another reason I still go out there and do the job, so when I am delivering training and some clever cunt says "How do you know what would happen?".....I can say "Cos I do this every Friday and Saturday night mate......that's how"!

The Beginning.

Life on the doors began in 1989……..

I was a young nineteen year old, living with my first wife, and my first baby daughter; (yes, I started young!) in a shabby two bedroom flat in the North East of England.

Being an apprentice plasterer; I wasn't making much money (The YTS scheme back then was £24.50 a week), so when a pal of mine, Darren, knocked on my door asking if I would work on a door in Wallsend with him I jumped at the chance. I was skint and couldn't afford to go out at weekends anyway, so I thought why not?

There were no interviews or applications back then….you got a start through either recommendation or reputation. Not like nowadays, where you do your course, pay for your license and then you're a "Door Supervisor". Back then, you could be pretty sure most door staff could have a fight, as that's why they had been asked to work there. The management knew they could deal with any shit, and their mates on the door with them knew they would be there for them in a scrap.

The bar was called the Carrville, (Re named Harry's Bar….after the owners father / grandfather) and was located at the bottom end of Wallsend (referring to it being situated at the end of Hadrians Wall), across the road from the local shipyards.

The proprietor wanted to hold karaoke nights, with bar

staff in bikinis etc, and had been advised to have door staff on the relevant nights.

Now I wasn't big, and I wouldn't say I was hard either; I had played rugby and boxed from a young age, so didn't mind the physical contact side of things. I knew could hit and be hit, I didn't have a clue how to go on as a doorman, but how hard could it be?

I rocked up that first night in my black trousers, white shirt, black v neck jumper and bow tie. I was told to stand on either door (there were two entrances – one either end of the bar), and if there was any bother we were to "sort it out"....that was our brief.

The locals, which was mainly what the bar consisted of, had never seen door staff there before, so we were quite a novelty attraction. We spent most of the first few nights fielding questions as to why we were there, was the owner expecting trouble etc?

To be fair in the short time we were there nothing really happened, so from an experience point of view I didn't really learn anything, apart from how to talk to customers etc. There were no conflict management modules or training courses back then, you went to work and learned on the job by watching the other experienced guys and making their methods your own.

There were three of us on the door, myself, Darren, and a guy called Mark. Mark always had flash cars, which he would always park nearby, and rumour has it that he used to keep a gun under the drivers seat....but that's another story!

It was at Harry's Bar where I had my first (and only) experience of my being a doorman getting me some female attention, and it was with a member of bar staff. Now my wife doesn't believe me, but I think the idea of all the girls wanting to shag you just because you're a doorman is a load of rubbish, it certainly has never been the case for me (except this one time); maybe I'm just too miserable, or too fucking ugly!

The money soon ran out for the owner of the venue, and as usual we were the first to go. Even though I hadn't done much (as in violence / confrontation) on that door, I was now known locally as a "bouncer", and my next offer of door work soon came along.

Whitley Bay

Another pal of mine was working in a bar in Whitley Bay; and asked if I wanted to come along and give him a hand on the door he was working on.

Whitley Bay is a coastal town not far from Newcastle, once renowned for its "strip" (South Parade), legendary all day bank holiday sessions, and a favourite of stag and hen parties. Unfortunately a lot of the venues in Whitley Bay have closed now; and the place isn't what it used to be anymore. The local planners and residents seem determined to make it an area of apartments, residential care homes and sea front restaurants.

A lot of parties still turn up from around the country, realize it is shit now, and then jump in a taxi to Newcastle.

The venue was called Dunes; and was situated on the lower promenade at the bottom of the main strip, and it was part owned by the brother of Sting, the lead singer of the band "The Police".

It was at Dunes where I first started to get my hands dirty, and had my first run in with the police (the real police.....not the band!)

The building was long, with three doors, one central entry / exit door, and fire exit doors at either end of the frontage....inside was a long bar, with a DJ stand and small dance floor at one end, and toilets at the other.

It was New Years Eve; the bar was chocka (really busy),

and I was on the main door, when the toilet fire exit door alarm went off.

I pushed through the crowd; and seen a guy repeatedly trying to open the fire exit door, which he couldn't open fully, as it kept catching on the thick textured ceiling (luckily there were never any fires there), which he was gradually scraping off every time he was tugging at the door.

I tried to pull him away from the door, and told him to go and use the main door, to which he replied "Fuck off....I'm going this way" and grabbed the door handle again; I pulled him away again and he went for me, grabbing my shirt and trying to head butt me.

It was so crowded he couldn't get a decent shot in; but I lost it.....I had been in a few scrapes by then and should have known better....but the old red mist came down, and off I went....

I grabbed him by the throat with one hand, pinning him to the wall, and writhed at the door handle until the door opened. I threw him out, and down towards the ground, he spun round and lunged back towards me, half bent over.

Instinctively I kicked out and caught him on the chin with my size 11 Doc Martens, everything then went into slow motion; his head went back and his body straightened, he then carried on backwards, toppling over like a felled tree until his head hit the concrete, sounding like a snooker ball being dropped on the ground.

A crowd immediately formed around him, as soon as somebody is knocked out inside or outside a venue, loads of nurses who are out on the drink appear. Fuck knows where they all come from, but there are always numerous cries of "I'm a nurse", and more recently we get a lot of punters declaring "I'm a first aider", and "I'm an army medic". I'm a first aider; and a first aid instructor, and often have to tell these pissed idiots to fuck off out of the way so we can sort the issue out, as all they do is get in the way.

Anyway, he lay on his back, legs twitching, but nothing else; then the twitching stopped, and he lay there lifeless.

To be honest I thought he was dead.

It seemed to take an age for the ambulance to get there, and when it did he was taken away and spent a few days in hospital.

The police took me in for statements etc, and I was advised that if he died I would likely face a charge of manslaughter, and a prison sentence.

For days I was shitting myself, I had a young family, and couldn't afford a police record, never mind going to jail. There was no CCTV back in those days, so it was all down to our statements and witness statements….luckily some customers had come forward and said what a dickhead he was being, and how he had went for me first when I had tried to move him away from the door. We also found out he was an off duty soldier, so my solicitor played on the impact it would have on his job if it went to court etc, and his behaviour was brought to light.

While all of this was going on, and I was on bail, I was still working. One night a guy kicks off and gets in my face, I didn't want to smack him, as I was still reeling a bit from past events, and conscious that I am currently on bail.

I try to push the guy away, and somehow he gets the ball of my thumb in his mouth, which he bites down on….hard….and it fucking hurts.

Now I don't want to start smacking the guy in case he rips my thumb off, and the other lads can't pull him away from me, in case my thumb goes with him. One of the lads ends up strangling him from behind until he lets go of my thumb, and then one of the other lads punched him on the chin and knocked him out, before he could bite anybody else.

I'm not a fan of biters, in another incident in Tynemouth,

someone tried to bite my face while we were grappling (Which is mentioned later, in another chapter). Another time I had fifteen stitches to stitch my right earlobe back on, which was almost bitten off in a nightclub incident.

Biting during fights seemed to die off a bit over the years (wherever I worked, anyway), but then a kid bit part of someone's ear off outside a nightclub I was working at recently. The police came back a few times looking for it, but as far as I know they never found it.

After a couple of weeks the charges were dropped, the reason given was that he didn't want to potentially adversely affect his military career by having the incident on his record. Some say he had a few home visits from a couple of people who weren't very nice as well....but who knows?

Tynemouth

I stayed at Dunes for a while, but eventually ended up migrating into a town call Tynemouth.

Tynemouth is a couple of miles away from Whitley Bay, and is on the same coastline, it is very picturesque with some castle ruins (the Priory); little tea shops, and bed and breakfasts.

Like Whitley Bay Tynemouth has its "strip", which is basically the main street, called "Front Street, Tynemouth"; which has a selection of bars running down either side.

Back then, along one side there was the Cumberland arms, the Percy, Fitzy's, and the Turks Head. On the other side there was The Salutation Inn (or The Sal), Berties, Oz's, The Furry Pear (the last two were in a little alley just off Front Street) and at the end was Sammy Jacks....an old converted church.

The weekends in Tynemouth always followed pretty much the same pattern, Fridays and Saturdays were always steady with older singles / couples, and then Sunday was always the busy night. This was still in the era of half eleven closing times, so we would usually start work around seven thirty, and work till around midnight.

I started off working at the Percy, which was historically the first or second bar people would go to when they were drinking in Tynemouth. The bar was usually busy until around nine o clock, and then dead thereafter....which often made it a long night.

As it was a "starter bar" the customers were rarely drunk or troublesome, so the shifts there usually passed quietly. I worked there with a gentle giant of a man called Richard, who unfortunately went home one Christmas eve and apparently passed away sat at his kitchen table while his wife was at work.....tragedy.

From the Percy I moved across the road to Sammy Jacks.

We had a good team at Sammy's, there was me, Morgan, Chris, and the company owner Stan....who still works the doors at sixty one (at time of writing).

You entered Sammy's via some stone steps, once inside you went up another flight of stairs to the ground floor, another flight to the dance floor area, and then another flight to the toilets; as you can imagine we dreaded kick offs around the toilets. It's no fun running up three flights of stairs, scrapping, and then trying to drag them out back down three flights of stairs.

There was a Chinese restaurant next door to Sammy's, and the owner would send us little bits of food round in exchange for sorting out any troublesome customers. We would drink tea on the door as well, but not just any old tea, but Earl Grey tea....cos we were posh doormen!

I'm on with Morgan (who is a right greedy bastard) one night, and the restaurant sends us some mini spring rolls over. Morgan starts eating his, while I sort something out at the front door, with Morgan behind me munching on his spring rolls and drinking his earl grey.

Anyway, I finish what I am doing and turn around to eat my share. I pick one up and bite into it.

"Fucking hell......there's no filling in this spring roll!"

"Mine were fine" says Morgan.....

I try the second one, no filling.....so I try the third and fourth.....no filling in any of them...

"Fucking bastards" I moan...."Not one of them had any

filling in them….can you believe it?"

I'm in a right huff by now, and am stomping round with a proper strop on.

After a few minutes huffing and puffing about my shit spring rolls, I notice Morgan bouncing up and down….trying not to laugh and spit his tea out.

"What you fucking laughing at?"

Turns out while I was sorting that stuff out on the door….he had bitten little holes in my spring rolls, sucked all the filling out, and then put the "rolls" back in the tray…..greedy bastard!!

We all had radios at all the different venues which were linked to the police; and you could alert the police at the push of a button.

If the button was pushed an operator would come on and ask the relevant venue if they required assistance, this would be broadcast on every radio in every venue; at which time most of the door staff on Front Street would leg it to the venue where the trouble was.

This one night the police came on

"Cumberland Arms, do you require assistance?"

Sammy Jacks was right across the road from The Cumberland (which didn't have door staff, but the bar staff / manager had a radio)…..we looked at each other and ran across the road.

Two of us burst in through the front door and into the main bar, nothing, not even a single customer! Within seconds about ten big lumps in black coats were stood in the bar bumping into each other, we ran through the back room, nobody there either?

Someone asks the bar staff "Where's the manager?"

"In the Cellar" she replies……

So the ten of us charge through the cellar door and down into the cellar….where the manager is sitting (on his radio….oblivious to the fact he has pushed the alert button)…..and he turns around to see ten of us glaring at him…puffing and panting.

"Fucks sake lads"…he says "What's going on?"……..

Exit ten pissed off doormen!

One night we refused entry to a very unassuming lad, slightly built, glasses on, but very drunk!

He wouldn't have it that he was too drunk, and wouldn't move away from the door, it got to the point where I had to physically take him down the stone steps to the wrought iron gates at the entrance.

Once at the entrance he grabbed at me and took a swing. I ducked the punch and tucked my chin in, looking up to see what he was doing, and that's when I saw his teeth. He was grabbing for my head and moving in to bite me.

Fuck that I thought, and threw a right uppercut which caught him nicely on the chin.

His head went back, his glasses flew off, and down he went….I had been in the game long enough by then to know when to stop. I looked down at him then walked back to the door, leaving him for his mates to pick up.

Another common practice at the time was using peoples heads and faces to open doors while you were escorting them out. We had knocked this guy and his mate back a couple of times one night, and then later on noticed he had sneaked into the bar; well to me that was just taking the piss! I went in and told him to fuck off….well the cheeky bastard just laughed at me, which made me even more annoyed.

I got behind him, just slightly to his right hand side and grabbed his arms, walking him quickly towards the double doors which led to the stairs and the way out. The doors were quite big, thick, heavy wooden things with long metal handles….and were closed. As we approached the doors I put my left hand on the back of his neck and bent him forward slightly, his face connected with the door and it flew open with a bang (luckily they opened outwards from the bar). I drove him down the stairs and out of the front door, Morgan had jumped out of the way so he didn't spill his tea, and I carried on dragging the guy down the concrete steps outside. He was starting to struggle and I was getting more and more pissed off with him. At the bottom of the steps I threw him onto the ground and stood over him, I had lost it and was seeing the old red mist. I raised my foot to stamp on his head and Morgan jumped down the stairs, pushing me away. I went to jump back in and Morgan grabbed me…"Fucking calm down man…dickhead" he said, and ushered me back up the stairs "Go and finish ya tea".

Morgan picked him up, and he wandered across the road onto the grassed area outside, he then spent ages shouting down his mobile phone, telling people where he was and arranging for people to come and shoot us. At one point his phone actually rang while he was shouting down it, but nobody ever did turn up to shoot us, he just wandered off eventually to the chip shop, and then passed a little while later, throwing chips at us.

During my time at Sammy's I went "back to school"….I was working as a finishing foreman for a large construction company, and went to night classes to gain my Foundation Degree in Construction Inspection and Control.

This was quite a testing time. I was at work every day, Monday to Saturday, at college on a Monday and Wednesday night, and then working the doors on a Friday, Saturday and Sunday night….leaving me a Tuesday and Thursday night at home, which were usually spent doing college work.

Needless to say I was knackered, and my partner (Donna, who is now my wife) was less than impressed.

From Sammy's I got moved round to Oz's bar, in the Alleyway….I spent my last few months in Tynemouth there and then had a little break from the industry.

I had secured a management role with a company during the day, which involved me going out to meetings with clients etc, and the company (who were high profile within their industry) didn't want me potentially turning up for meetings with black eyes etc.

Unfortunately, I still turned up for my first day on the new job with two black eyes……..

My last night in Tynemouth ended prematurely with my first experience of a sucker punch.

I was working in the alleyway at Oz's bar, with a doorman I won't name as he is still working in the industry, but those who were around at the time know who he is….and for the tale we will call him Bob (not his real name).

Anyway; Bob and I are on the door, and Bob is quite a big lad who talks a good show, and is apparently quite hard. This kid comes up with tracksuit bottoms on; and Bob whispers to me not to let him in with them on…"Sorry bud…you can't come in with them on" I says, pointing at his tracksuit bottoms. He isn't impressed by this as apparently he has been in before with tracksuit bottoms on, and doesn't see why he can't come in this time….I just shrug my shoulders and tell him it's against the bars dress code.

He carries on moaning for a bit and then Bob steps forward…. "Go on mate, just go in" he says. Well now I'm confused. A few minutes later the owner comes out and tells me there's a guy in the bar with tracksuit bottoms on, and can I get him out. I look at Bob, and Bob turns away from me and the owner. I went in and walked the guy out, of course when he gets outside he kicks off because he doesn't know what the fuck is going on, first he can't go in, then he can, now I say he can't again. Not surprisingly he thinks I'm taking the piss out of him.

He starts jumping around outside on his toes like a boxer, calling me outside into the alleyway. In hindsight I should have stayed on the door, let him jump around for a bit, get bored and go away....but not back then. I stepped down from the door and moved towards him, hands up, chin tucked in. I got in close and could feel him punching against my arms. I could hear Bob shouting "Leave them to it…it's a one on one"…and I'm thinking "Hang on a fucking minute…shouldn't you be out here with me trying to stop this kid fighting?"

I start throwing punches over the top, and it doesn't take long for them to connect, knocking the guy against a car parked in the alleyway, which I pin him against. I carry on punching until a couple of his mates get between us and I back off, with that he runs off up the alleyway towards the main street. There is a bar just around the corner, so we go to warn the door staff not to let this guy in as he has been fighting etc, but nobody has seen him?

We are standing talking to the lads outside the bar when BANG!... I saw the old white flash and fell against the metal shutters of the shop next to the bar. Straight away I put my hands up and stepped forward. I was rocked but I composed myself and looked through my hands…there he was, the guy from the alley, with a knuckleduster on. It all happened so fast, and once he saw he hadn't knocked me out, and before anybody could grab him, he fucked off up the street. I was in no condition to chase him, and nobody else could be bothered, so off he went.

I went round and sat on the steps of the fire exit, and my pal John came round from Berties bar to give me some first aid. The blow from the knuckleduster had broke my nose, and it also had a split in the side of it (I still have the scar). Now my nose is big and bumpy enough, so this didn't do it any favours. I couldn't stay at work as I needed a couple of butterfly stitches, so I walked to my car to take myself to hospital. On the way I passed Sammy Jacks, where I worked with Morgan, who was less than impressed when he saw my face and heard the tale of how Bob had stirred everything up and then stood back. I have worked with a number of guys like that, they will wind people up and create conflict, but then step back when it kicks off and gets physical. Unfortunately despite being found out and exposed, they still manage to find work in the industry.

A Normal Life?

Somehow I had managed to stumble onto the career ladder like most normal, sensible people do. While doing some agency plastering work for a construction company I was asked by their director if I would do some work in some properties he was renovating, the same guy then approached me with an offer of a finishing foreman role on a housing contract they had just begun.

I accepted, but didn't have a clue what I was doing. Here I was on a big building site, overseeing all of these experienced builders and inspecting their work, when in reality I didn't even know what I was looking at! The Director would ring up for progress reports and I would be saying things like "Erm; plot fifteen…the pointy wooden things are on, but there are no tiles on the roof yet"….he would then talk me through the relevant terminology and what should happen next etc.

Whilst in that role I began a foundation degree in Construction Inspection and Control (Clerk of Works Degree) as mentioned earlier.

The client who we were building for then offered me a role as a Contracts Manager / Clerk of Works for them, but one condition was that I stopped working as a doorman……I was with them for a couple of years, and then our kitchen supplier offered me a role as Contracts Director, which I took.

That lasted for another three years, but then with the crash of the housing market the company went into insolvency and closed. I thought I had it made for the last few years, good salaries, company cars, expense accounts and pension, it had been good but now I was out of a job. There was only one thing for it; I leased a van and went back on the tools….and back on the doors.

It was fun while it lasted….and I had had a nice break, but fuck me it was boring!

Whilst on my "break" I still did the odd cover shift, and private function, just to keep my hand in.

One such private party was in the grounds of a big house on the outskirts of Newcastle for a students birthday.

The owner of the house didn't want the students going into the house and using the toilets, or fucking around being a nuisance around the perimeter wall of the grounds and upsetting the neighbours.

We were tasked with mincing around the grounds, keeping them away from the perimeter wall, and just making sure they behaved themselves in general.

So we are patrolling around the perimeter wall and it's starting to get dark, we notice this black guy in a suit leaning against the chest high perimeter wall, looking out over it.

"Mate, you can't stand there" we call to him.

He turns his head, and gestures for us to be quiet, and to give him two minutes!

With that we look down and spot a pair of knees between his legs…..he is only standing there getting a blow job!!

"Two minutes" we say, and walk off.

A short time later we are walking around the inside of the grounds where there is a central feature of a circular brick wall, with some flowers etc in it, and there's the same black guy giving it to some bird from behind (a different bird from the blow job incident earlier)….we watch for a little bit (to check he isn't hurting her), then give him a shout…..he puts his cock away laughing and wanders off.

We go back to the same spot a little later, and the dirty fucker is there again, this time getting another blow job from another different bird; now bear in mind there are no toilets for this guy to wash his dick in, so in-between all this sucking and fucking his dick hasn't been washed once….dirty bastard.

He was quite proud of himself to be fair, and even came to find us with some of his mates before they left to confirm his story, as they didn't believe he had sex and blow jobs from three different girls that night.

At one point the owner gave us a shout as people couldn't get in one of the portaloos, after some banging and tugging on the door…it opens to reveal some bird in a policewoman costume straddling some guy….everybody cheered….she climbed off, grinned, pulled her knickers up and carried on partying….we get some proper classy students in Newcastle!

Once a year a travelling fairground used to come to Newcastle called the Town Moor.

The local bars in Jesmond and Gosforth used to be shitting themselves as they expected the travelers from the fair to pop in, get pissed, and then smash their bars and customers up. I was asked if I would work with another guy on a bar called The Brandling in Gosforth, to protect it and its customers from the marauding travelers.

The bar was dead all night until about nine thirty, when two young lads who had been working the fairground came in with a couple of girls. They sat in the corner with their pockets full of pound coins spending and drinking as much as they could before the bar closed, and they were no bother at all.

I have came across countless members of the travelling community in my time, in both pubs and nightclubs, and to date I have never had any trouble with them. They will usually speak to you at the door, shake your hand and offer you a drink, they will then go in and keep themselves to themselves. If they do get in bother they tend to police themselves, and a couple of times I have ran into scraps and they have been by my side, punching people and mucking in with the door staff!

I had decided when I left the doors at Tynemouth that I would never return to the coast full time, it was a bit local for me, and always seemed to be the same crowd, stood in the same place at the same time. I was going to go and play with the big boys in the city centre.

I knew a couple of guys who worked on the doors for both the bigger firms in the town and some of the smaller in house groups, and a pal of mine had lined me up a start on the door he was working on, for a group who had a small number of bars in the city centre. I had also been offered a start in a local casino…..but then something else cropped up!

For years I had been having palpitations and little heart flutters but never thought anything of it....I was reasonably fit and could run and train, so I thought it was just one of those things and got on with it.

Around the time I decided to go and work the doors in the city centre I was back on the tools, plastering and tiling. I'd been feeling a bit rough at work for a few days, puffing and panting and sweating all the time, at one point I stood in a client's garden and nearly passed out....I just put it down to needing a rest, and planned in a few days off.

Anyway, I got up one morning and felt really hung over, I went into the bathroom and sat on the edge of the bath; the room was spinning, I was sweating but I was cold, my whole body was shaking.... "fucking hell' I thought... "this isn't right!

I arranged to see the doctor, who thought it may be an issue with my thyroid, but to cover all the bases she advised I go to my local hospital for an ECG to get my heart checked etc....

I turned up at the hospital and whipped my top off for the nurse to put all the wires and sticky pads on me, I was due to work on a casino that night....so was hoping it wouldn't take long. Anyway she turns the machine on and looks at the monitor with a raised eyebrow....."Are you taking any drugs?" She asks...

"No"....I replied

"Steroids?" Was her next question......

"Nope"......

"Wait there.....I'll be right back"....and with that she disappeared around the curtain.

I really wasn't expecting what happened next.....she came back in with a wheelchair and told me to get in it.... "I'm fine"..I said.. "I'll just walk"

"No you won't".....she replied.... "get in"

She wheeled me round to the ECU (Emergency care unit) and put me on a bed, I was then wired to a portable heart monitor and had a cannula put in my hand.....I was shitting myself....I thought I would have been home drinking tea by now, instead all these nurses were running around sticking things in and on my body.

After a short while this guy popped in to see me and had a chat about my symptoms etc. He explained what he thought was wrong with me. Turns out I had a condition called Atrial Fibrillation, which occurs when the top two chambers of the heart beat erratically and can result in blood clots, which can then cause a stroke or embolism if they go into your bloodstream.....so now I was really shitting myself!

He explains the first course of treatment is to put a drug straight into my heart via a tube in the vein in my arm. I laughed as I thought he was kidding....he wasn't. He wandered off for a bit and then came back in all his green surgeons kit, with about six foot of tubing rolled up under his arm....well if my heart was beating erratically before it was going fucking berserk now I can tell you!

Anyway he sits down and puts this tube in my arm, which

apparently went all the way to my heart, and then the drug (Amiodarone) was pumped in from a drip stand.... It didn't work.

I was told the next step was to undergo a procedure called a cardioversion, which is where they sedate you, put the sticky pads on your chest, and then stop and restart your heart via an electric shock, a bit like re booting a computer. As you can imagine I wasn't too fucking thrilled at this prospect either. Before I could undergo the procedure I had to be on beta blockers and anti clotting drugs for a period of time, this was to ensure no blood clots were released into my bloodstream, and that if they were they would be broken down and not fuck me up. I was in hospital for three days getting jabbed and getting medication levels sorted out. It was a very long weekend!

Before being discharged I had a chat with the consultant, who categorically advised against my returning to work as a doorman until things were sorted out, as if I got wounded and was bleeding, the anti coagulant drugs I was taking would mean the bleeding wouldn't stop....which wouldn't be good for me....bleeding everywhere!

Anyway, being the arrogant arsehole I am, I shook his hand, walked out of the hospital, and phoned my pal to tell him I was available for work.

Mushroom

Mushroom is a bar situated underground in Newcastle City Centre; and my pal Fred was head doorman there, Fred and I had met many years ago when we both boxed at a local boxing club as boys. As we got older and moved into the door scene, Fred went to work in the town and I went to work down the coast. It used to be rumoured that Mushroom had one of the longest bars in a city centre venue, I don't know about that, but it was certainly one of the busiest.

I had to go up and see Fred on a Sunday evening, to sign the relevant paperwork, produce my license and meet the manager etc. I turned up and met a guy called Geoff on the door. Fred was inside apparently, so I introduced myself, and Geoff got on the radio to tell Fred I was there. Fred and I went downstairs to the office and met Micky the manager. Micky was great fun, he would always be beside you if you needed him, and he liked nothing more than standing upstairs with us asking punters for ID, which was often met with comments like "who are you like?" and "Do you work here?"....as he didn't look or dress like a doorman. Many a time we had to stand in between him and punters who were getting irate with him. From the front door on the main street you entered a small lobby with a double set of glass doors; in one corner was the monitor for the cctv which allowed us to see what was going on downstairs. Through the double doors you turned left and headed down a short flight of stairs; then doubled back on yourself to go down another flight of stairs and into the bar. The venue was basically a long room; with a bar down the full length of the right hand side, and seating areas and toilets on the left hand side. A small dance floor and DJ stand were in the far left hand corner; and the office was in the far right hand corner.

We went through the formalities and signed all of the relevant forms. We went through the working hours, rates of pay and where we signed in etc. They told me how it was generally quiet in the bar and there wasn't much trouble, despite it being a busy venue. We all shook hands and Fred and I headed back upstairs. As we walked along the length of the bar on our way out; Fred grabbed a guy who was dancing like a pissed giraffe, spilling and splashing drink everywhere. Fred walked him upstairs, out of the bar and into the street….while Fred was tucking himself in again a taxi pulled up outside and two guys got out….Fred pointed at one of them and said "And you can get lost….you're not coming in ya barred". The guy stood and argued for a bit and then fucked off….shouting he was gonna come back and do us all in etc (as they do).

Geoff said nothing; just looked me, Fred looked at me and grinned. "Told you it was quiet, didn't I?"......I just laughed….in a couple of nights I would be working there.

My first few nights came and went without real incident, there were the usual punters who were too pissed or asleep who had to be brought out of the bar, but apart from that there was no real trouble. Most of the confrontation was at the front door when people were told they couldn't come in, one of the team Davey, was a big mountain of a man; and normally being told to fuck off by him was enough…not many argued with him….they just did as they were told and fucked off.

One week night when me and Davey were on the front

door we had a stag do (or birthday – can't remember, we'll call it a stag do) in, which had a few doormen amongst it, one of which worked for the same group as us. There was also an older, ex doorman in the bar who was a bit of a legend…and who was a proper fighter. Anyway this older door lad is having a domestic outside with a lady friend, and one of the stag do comes outside for a smoke and involves himself in it….now from where we were standing it looked like they were all chatting….until the older door lad clips the other guy on the chin and knocks him out cold!

With this he walks towards the door and holds out his hand "Sorry about that lads…I'm off" he says, shaking our hands and walking off down the street….in the meantime one of sleeping beauty's pals has been out and seen him unconscious on the pavement….and ran in to get his mates.

A bunch of them come thundering out the door and run along the street after the older door lad, now you would expect him to take his to heels and run away from the six or so guys bearing down on him…but not this guy, fuck that, not his style. He turns to face them and adopts a fighting stance, hands up, chin tucked in, and starts punching.

Despite his bravery it didn't take long before he was on the ground, and they were trying to kick his head in. Now while on his feet it was a bit of a fair fight, but not now that he was on the ground. Me and Davey ran over and got mixed up in it….just the sight of Davey running over convinced some of them to step back. The guy we worked with was on older guys back, and trying to hook his arm under his chin to get a choke on, so I jumped on his back to try and pull him off. I took a couple of sly kicks to the head (I think they were aiming for older guy) while I was in amongst it….we noticed the street cctv camera had turned to where we were rolling about, so everybody seen sense and fucked off before the police turned up.

Older guy came back to the bar with us and went down to the toilets to clean himself up. He came up with a few bumps and scratches but didn't look too bad considering, he shook our hands again and fucked off for more drinks, and no doubt to see if he could find any guys from that stag do to roll around with again.

Quilted Camel

The Quilted Camel is a bar on Newcastle's quayside, and is next to one of the oldest and most historic buildings in Newcastle, Bessie Surtess House. The buildings which contain Bessie Surtees House and The Quilted Camel are made up of several wealthy merchants' houses, built in the 16th and 17th centuries. Since that time these houses have been used as a hide-out for smugglers, thieves and prostitutes, and have also been the scene of some heinous acts including displaying the butchered remains of villains who crossed the laws of the day. Apparently the main bar at The Quilted Camel was a renowned brothel in the 18th century. It was also a home for abandoned children at one time, and apparently the cries of children could be regularly heard by a member of staff in parts of the venue when it was quiet.

The venue consists of two bars (and a vip area) situated on one floor, the first floor of the building, which is accessed through a set of double doors and up a flight of stairs. Its name derives from a pilot covering the wings of his Sopwith Camel aeroplane with quilts to allow him to prevent the wings of his plane icing up....you wouldn't believe the amount of times we tell that story to curious customers!

There would only ever be two of us working at the Camel, which wasn't always ideal as it catered for a lot of stag and birthday groups, and a lot of out of town groups who were up for the weekend. You would both be stood on the main door with a radio, and there would be a radio upstairs in the bar, every now and again one of us would go for a walk around inside, and there was a cctv monitor down by the front door so we could keep an eye on the customers upstairs.

I was working there one Bank Holiday Sunday with David, who I had worked on a couple of different nightclubs with before. We were doing a long shift with it being a Bank Holiday, and it was busy. David went for a walk around inside and I was standing looking for him on the monitor. I saw him stand amongst a group of lads and stick his arms out, separating them. I ran upstairs and over to where they were in the main bar. David indicated that a group of around seven of them were kicking off, so I turned and ushered three of them towards the staircase, sensing that David was behind me ushering some of the others out.

As we got half way down the stairs the three guys in front of me stopped, and the ones behind me with David stood close to me, trapping me between the two groups. It took me a second to realise I was in the shit and this was going to go bad!....There was no time for conflict management, I was gonna get fucked on the stairs here, so I put my head down and charged forward, one guy had a hold of the metal handrail, so I grabbed his thumb and bent it backwards, forcing him to let go.

We all went stumbling down the stairs and landed in a heap at the bottom, Micky and another manager Steve had joined us and we were pushing kids out the door onto the street. Just then David came rolling out the door with some guy wrapped around him. David was on top but this guy wasn't letting go, so I bent over, reached down and grabbed the guys bollocks...and squeezed, hard.

I felt the impact to my face and got the old white flash briefly, as I was bending over grabbing his bollocks, one of his pals had run up and kicked me in the face. I heard and sensed it more than felt it, I was full of adrenaline so didn't feel a thing. I looked up and the kicker was standing squaring up to me, I think he was a little shocked I hadn't went down, but just straightened up and looked at him…. "Is that the best you've got"? I said to him as I stepped towards him. I was a little dazed but I wasn't going to show it, and I could hear Micky on the radio somewhere asking for police assistance.

Anyway they all fucked off and apparently the police were tracking them on the cctv. I went back on the door and spent the rest of the night dabbing the seeping cut on my nose, and fielding questions about what happened….and to this day we are still waiting for the police to turn up!

Another night we had a pretty nasty glassing in the bar. We got a shout on the radio to go to the DJ stand. When I got there I noticed the Perspex screen around the top of the booth had splashes of blood on it, as did the DJ's shirt….he was less than impressed as the shirt was new. The DJ pointed to some guy who was bent over with his hand over his eye; at this point we didn't know he had been glassed.

I asked him to move his hand so I could see any damage, expecting a bit of a shiner and a cut….well fuck me it was horrible!….he had a big crescent shaped gash around his eye, and some of the skin from the side of his nose was flapping about, "Fucking hell mate"…I said "Put ya hand back on it"! We took him downstairs and one of the managers gave him first aid until the ambulance came for him and took him away. The poor bugger was from Holland or somewhere and had came over for the weekend….one of the last things you expect on a weekend away is to nearly lose your eye!

We were finishing off one night and I was down at the front door while the other doorman was upstairs ushering people out etc. as it was the end of the night we had a bit of a crowd outside and a few hanging around the door, and then this tall guy tries to go upstairs.

"Sorry mate we're closing, nobody else is going in" I says…."But my mates are inside" he replies……

"They'll be down in a minute…everyone's coming down now" I tell him.

Anyway, he demands to go upstairs as he is looking for some dwarves, as funny as that sounds some dwarves had been in earlier so it did make a bit of sense. I told him they had left, and he wasn't going up stairs regardless.

So then he tried to walk past me, I put my left hand out and stopped him, holding him back…"Told you already mate…you're not going in"….he steps closer and is right up to my face this time, with his forehead pressing against mine….fuck this I thought!

I pushed forward against his forehead, and then physically pushed him off with two hands. I didn't push him hard, but he was falling backwards, and kept going and going.

Some poor girl was standing by the roadside looking at her phone; oblivious to what was going on….he bumped into her and knocked her on her arse in the middle of the road….a taxi had to swerve to avoid hitting her, which in turn almost hit a passing police car, which had to swerve to avoid the taxi….

Two policemen got out of their car just as the girls boyfriend started getting stuck into the guy who I had pushed, and who had then knocked his girlfriend over. People were shouting at me for pushing him, saying it was all my fault, she was sat in the road crying because her bum hurt and her phone was smashed, her boyfriend was kicking off with the police, and the guy I had pushed was kicking off because he had been assaulted, to top it off the whole road was blocked with the police car and taxis, who were all moaning and tooting their horns!

It was all getting a bit mad so I fucked off upstairs and sent the other lad downstairs. After closing we watched the cctv footage a couple of times, it wasn't funny at the time, but it just shows how quickly things can escalate.

Perdu

Perdu is owned by the same group who own Mushroom and the Quilted Camel, so you could often find yourself working at any of the three venues, and is situated on an area of Newcastle known as the Diamond Strip, which is one of the busiest parts of Newcastle, but also attracts the most posers and dickheads.

It was while working at Perdu one night that I first felt the impact of my heart condition.

I was standing up on the DJ stand, which had some booths opposite with round tables in, which seated around six to eight people. In between the DJ stand and the booths was a bit of a dance floor area, about ten feet wide, which was also a causeway for people moving from the front to the back of the venue.

I noticed two guys kicking off outside one of the booths. I stepped down from the DJ stand and ran towards them, calling it in is as I went "Door staff to DJ stand, door staff to DJ stand", hoping that when the lads ran in they would either see me or the DJ would point them in the right direction.

At Perdu we normally have two on the front door, one on the stage, one on the DJ stand, and two on both of the back doors....with that many guys I was sure the cavalry wouldn't take long to turn up.

The two guys were in a pretty tight clinch, so rather than

try and pull them apart I threw them both to the ground, together. As they went down I landed on top of them; so we were now stacked three high, the guy on the bottom was on his back, the guy in the middle was still facing him, and I was on his back on top.

The guy on the bottom realizes I'm a doorman and puts his hands out, the guy in the middle starts shouting "Fucking get off me" and puts his hands on the floor, in a press up position, and starts lifting himself off the ground, with me on his back. This guy was a big strong fucker; and I'm thinking "If he gets up here with me on his back I'm fucked".....by now I'm also thinking "Where's the fucking door staff?"

With that I look to my left and see a pair of black boots running over, but then they turn right and run away from me, off to the other side of the dance floor, where I later learned something else had kicked off... "Shit" I thought!

I couldn't risk letting this guy get up with me on his back so I slipped my arm under his chin to put a choke on. Now I don't like using chokes as I'm not practiced in them....but I thought "fuck it...just copy what the other lads do"......I hooked my arm around and squeezed....nothing, he was still getting up, he had his knee bent and underneath him now....so I squeezed harder, he softened a little and fell back on the poor guy at the bottom...."Thank fuck for that" I thought.

Then he tensed up and started getting up again, "For fucks sake" I thought, I abandoned the choking option and rolled off him, jumping up so I was standing in front of him as he stood up, before he straightened up I grabbed his shirt with my right hand and smashed the heel of my left hand into his chin....rocking him, I then half walked and half dragged him to the front door and down the three or four concrete steps outside, I then let him go, and stood back.

Well I was a right mess, my shirt was hanging out, my tie was off, my radio was dangling down by my leg...I was puffing and panting and sweat was pissing out of me. He turned around and offered me his hand "Sorry mate....I didn't realize you were a doorman" he said smiling...he wasn't even out of breath!

I shook his hand, shook my head and went back in the club. I tucked myself in and then stood by the DJ's big cooling fan until I stopped sweating...I was there for fucking ages!

Not long after this my appointment came through for the cardioversion. I took a long weekend off as I was having the procedure on a Friday, and if all went according to plan I would be home on the Friday night, but it would take my body a few days to respond to the procedure.

I went into hospital and Donna came with me, we were in our own room and the consultant kept popping in to tell me about the procedure, what the risks were (dying was one of them), and I had to sign a form saying that nobody would complain if they stopped my heart and couldn't get it going again.

Anyway after a while they wheeled me along to theatre, it was like a production line, as I was going in others were coming out. A pretty nurse sat by my head and started making small talk while a couple of others put the pads on my body; and another one put a needle in the back of my hand....I looked at the pretty nurse and felt my hand go cold....that was it, I was gone.

I could hear the pretty nurses voice calling my name, I half opened my eyes and she started making small talk again, I was slurring back at her but god knows what I was saying...it must have been funny because she was laughing, or maybe just being polite?

I came round a bit more and then felt the bed begin to move. They were wheeling me back to my room and I remember thinking "My chest hurts".

We got back to the room and Donna was still there, apparently I had been away longer than expected because the procedure hadn't worked the first or second time. It had taken three attempts to get my heart going in a normal rhythm…"Bloody hell" I thought "My hearts been stopped twice". I kept thinking of the movie "Flatliners", where Kevin Bacon and his mates stop each others hearts and then see ghosts and all kind of weird shit, but unfortunately nothing like that happened to me, not that I can recall anyway.

They gave me a cup of tea and a couple of chocolate biscuits, and the consultant came in and asked me how I felt. To be fair I didn't feel any different, but he explained that it would take my body a few days to adjust to my heart rate being back to normal.

Once I got home I could notice the difference, I could walk the dogs and not be out of breath, I could go to bed and not wake up the next morning dripping with sweat and with cramps in my arms and hands. Every now and again my hands would shake uncontrollably, really bad, these symptoms were all linked to my heart condition, and now they had gone away.

I'm much more aware of my heart now and how to look after it. I regularly sit and check my pulse out of both habit and paranoia, and when I am delivering first aid training I give a very informative talk on angina and heart attacks….and atrial fibrillation.

And the weekend after, I was back on the door.

Tiger Tiger

Nobody worked at Mushroom, Perdu, or The Quilted Camel on a Tuesday, so every Tuesday I would go and work at Tiger Tiger; at an event called Koosdays. I was now working six nights a week as a doorman, so wasn't doing anything during the day.

Tiger Tiger is a nationwide brand, and the one in Newcastle is situated just next to the Gate complex and the Eldon Square shopping complex. It has a ground floor with a bar and restaurant, a first floor with a cloakroom and small bar, and a second floor which has a main bar with four other bars branching off that one....one of which is the white room.

The white room is what it is, a big white room, with a small stage at one end, a small stage in the middle, and two small bars at opposite sides of the room.

I was asked to run the white room one Halloween, which I didn't mind as it normally got a good crowd in, mainly students who were more aggravation than trouble.

Anyway this night was manic....everybody was in fancy dress, so the room was filled with sexy zombie nurses, schoolgirls, cheerleaders and some just in underwear with zombie make up on. Once the trouble started though it was like a fucking conveyor belt, to throw somebody out you had to get them into a fire exit, then call a manager, and then be accompanied as you took them down around eight flights of concrete steps to the ground floor exits.

Well all night long we were throwing out zombies, transformers, surgeons, superheroes, and people in morph suits. We were fucking knackered climbing up and down the stairs all night, but we had a bloody good laugh radioing through to the front door describing the different characters we were throwing out.

At one point they let some fireworks off above the central stage where I was standing, "We found Love" by Rhianna was playing, and the sparks came down and burned my arms. To this day that song still reminds me of that night.

Another night I was working in one of the smaller bars on the second floor, Groovy Koosdays, and I was standing on the small flight of steps leading up o the couple of VIP seating areas. I looked around at the seats and there was a girl sat between two blokes, the guy on her left had his cock out in her hand, and she was leaning over sucking the cock of the guy on her right!

It took me a while to comprehend what I was seeing, and for it to actually sink in. When it did I went across to them, no surprise the two guys were just sitting grinning at me…."Sorry guys you'll have to go" I said… "You too" I said to the girl, when she looked up.

"Come on mate….cant we just put our cocks away?" one of them contested, she just sat and had a sip of her drink. I admired their audacity but I made them leave anyway, god knows what they ended up doing.

The Dogs

After a while I moved on from Mushroom etc and ended up at Sunderland Greyhound Stadium (The Dogs).

This was mainly on a Friday and Saturday evening, and the shifts were from around six or seven o clock at night until one o clock the next morning. They were long hours, but at least you were getting home at a decent time.

There were normally four or five of us would work at the dogs, two would be trackside ensuring nobody took any glasses or bottles outside, and the rest would be upstairs where the main bar and restaurant was. Once all of the dog racing was finished the nightclub "Trapz" would open upstairs. Now the nightclub was an experience in itself, it was more like just a bar with very few lights, and its occupants were always a mixed bunch, as we often had works parties, birthdays there etc.

One downside of the venue was that it was a bit out of the way, so if you threw anybody out the furthest they could go was the car park....unless their car was in the car park, or their taxi was there they were stuck!

It was getting near Christmas so we were getting busy with the works Christmas outings, these usually consisted of people of all ages being in the club together; and most of the older ones who don't get out much making fools of themselves on the dance floor to the eighties classics and

Christmas favourites that the DJ played.

We were nearly finished one night and one of the lads, Ryan, was going around asking people to finish their drinks off. Now Ryan isn't the biggest of lads, but he can handle himself.

I was at the bar having a little drink of coke and I'm listening to Ryan asking people to finish off when I hear a guy to my right say "Fuck off….I'll finish when I'm ready"…..well I just knew that now he would be leaving before he finished that drink, so I put mine down and looked at Ryan.

"Get him out of here" Ryan said to me quietly.

This guy didn't look like your typical arsehole (if there is one), he was a big fella, just over six foot, in his late forties, and well built with glasses on….he was standing grinning smugly at the little crowd of men and women around him, and must of thought none of the door staff (who were all smaller than him) would challenge him.

"Come downstairs with me mate" I said, touching his right arm with my left hand.

"What for"? he asked…. "Because you're being abusive to the door staff, so you can go and wait downstairs for the rest of your group"…and with that I took his drink from his hand.

Anyway he started to walk, we had to go along a corridor and then down a couple of flights of stairs to get to the main foyer. As we were walking along the corridor he kept stopping and turning back to me, growling and posturing, a woman behind me was shouting after him, telling him not to start anything and just to go downstairs….I was beginning to think he had done this before.

I was walking behind him at arms length, and at one point he stopped and turned to face me, sticking his chest out and standing as tall as he could. I knew I was on cctv but that there was no audio, so I stuck my left hand (in a non aggressive stance) and said "Look ya fat cunt…I couldn't give a fuck if you want to fight…I get paid to fill cunts like you in every weekend….if you want it lets go"!….on cctv it would look like I was trying to diffuse the situation, but in reality I was ready to punch him right on the fucking chin!

He had a little think and then turned around and walked towards the stairs. I didn't know who was behind me, but I knew the lads would be there somewhere. We gets halfway down the first set of stairs and he turns on me and goes for it!

I'm expecting it, so I tucks my chin in, pushes into him and turns him against the wall, I actually backed him against another one of the team who was behind me on the stairs, who started restraining him. I'm pushing him back and I can feel blows to the back of my head, so I turn around and some guy (I presume a friend of his) is standing growling at me with his fists clenched. I grab him by the throat and pin him against the wall; punching him twice in the head…"Fuck off downstairs!" I shouted. He looked a little shocked, he must frequent one of those clubs where the door staff don't hit back, I thought to myself.

So he fucks off downstairs out of the way, and the big fella virtually gets thrown down the rest of the stairs, then gets up and walks out into the car park, glasses all wonky, shirt hanging out and everything. In the struggle I've got a cut head; one lad (we found out later) had a broken rib, and another broke a finger.

The police are already in the car park dealing with another incident, and the big fella starts moaning to them that he has been assaulted by the door staff….unbelievable!

People like that really piss me off; if they get the better of the door staff they are walking round, chest puffed out, putting shit all over Facebook etc….yet when they get filled in and embarrassed by the door staff nothing is said, apart from them crying to the police that the nasty doormen picked on them for nothing.

The police had to pursue it, and we all had to go down to

the police station and make statements, be photographed for ID parades and have fingerprints taken. Nothing ever came of it, we weren't told the charges had been dropped or otherwise, we just heard nothing more about it.

Cosy Joe's

Cosy Joe's is a karaoke bar situated in Newcastles Groat Market. For any of the older readers, it was also known as Rewind, and Maceys, downstairs is just a bar really, and upstairs is a smaller room with a bar and stage for karaoke; with a corridor containing a number of room, or party pods as they are called.

There is always a brilliant atmosphere in Cosy's, and I used to really like working there, but I hated karaoke. There was only one way in and out, so on busy nights we would have two on the front door, one keeping an eye on the inside, and one upstairs in the karaoke bar.

I ended up on the front door one "Black eye Friday", the Friday when the majority of businesses close for Christmas, and all of the once a year drinkers come to town and make fools of themselves, get filled in by other piss heads or door staff, and go home with black eyes!

Anyway I'm stood in the doorway with Rob and this guy who is blatantly smashed comes up to the door... "Sorry bud you can't come in….you've had too much already" I said politely. We then got in the usual conversation whereby he assured me he had not had too much to drink, which quickly escalated into me being an arsehole because I still wouldn't let him. He steps back and looks around for a bit, then gets his phone out and starts filming me on his phone. I put up with it for about ten seconds and then made a grab for his phone. Now I meant to grab it; but instead it flew out of his hand and smashed into pieces on the pavement….needless to say he wasn't impressed. He crawled around and retrieved all the pieces, and then stood about five feet away from the door, on the edge of the pavement in front of me….rocking backwards and forwards (but he reckoned he wasn't pissed!).

Me and Rob both knew what was coming, it was just a case of when….he was building himself up to have a go. We were both standing sniggering at each other, and watching him out of the corners of our eyes.

Well he went for it big style….a massive haymaker of a punch which was well telegraphed, I managed to step back out of his reach and the poor bloke fell forward onto the step, then he jumped up and ran off while me and Rob had a good laugh about it.

A little while later and he's back again, he must have walked around the block and now he is opposite the door on the other side of the road, a couple of regulars had been talking to him, and came across to warn me that he was gonna "Do me in"…..

We had a little queue at the door, with this big lump of a lad at the front, proper bodybuilder type, and by now the guy from across the street has come over the road and is mincing around outside the door again, right behind Mr. Bodybuilder.

Mr. Bodybuilder sees me watching this guy and asks me "Should I smack him for ya?"…. "No, no" I replied "He'll get bored and fuck off shortly"…..anyway about twenty seconds later Mr puncher throws another big haymaker, but this time it's a sucker punch at Mr Bodybuilders head….and he lands it smack on his right ear, then fucks off down the street….fast!

Me and Rob couldn't believe it; Mr Bodybuilder just shook his head and then fucked off after him, we heard a screech of tyres but didn't know what had happened. Turns out

Mr Puncher had ran down the street and across the road; whereby he ran into a car (hence the screeching of tyres), Mr Bodybuilder then caught up with him and gave him a good hiding in return for the sucker punch.

Another time we were called into the bar to get some guy who was asleep, he wasn't actually asleep he was just really pissed and lying against the bar. So I go over and give him a nudge "Come on mate...lets go outside" I said; and he stepped back from the bar...no dramas. Then this bloke appears; about my height, quite stocky and wearing glasses... "I'll take him" he says to me, and then lies him back against the bar.
"Come on then" I said "Take him outside"
"Yeah , yeah" he replies..... "In five minutes"
I glanced around and saw Rob was about eight feet away, looking on in case I needed him.
"No mate....now" I said....I was standing just behind him; behind his left shoulder, so I leant into him to get him moving....he tensed up and looked at me sideways.... Here we "o" I thought to myself.
He swung with his right hand and caught me in the face with two quick punches.... "Cheeky bastard" I thought to myself, as I stepped back and returned the favour with two big rights of my own, knocking him against the bar and onto the floor.
Both Rob and I were on him in an instant. I had him pinned by the throat, squeezing his carotid arteries, and Rob had his knee on his head....he was then dragged along the floor and put outside on the pavement...whereby the police had a chat with him and sent him on his way.
In all the commotion the guy sleeping at the disappeared....fuck knows where he went.
I don't normally work on my own, but one time I did was at Cosy Joe's.
It was a Saturday afternoon and Newcastle were playing away, we had the match on the screens in the bar but there

wasn't many in. I would be in by myself for a couple of hours and then the other lads would start coming in. I'm not a lover of football, so I just stood at the door in the fresh air.

One of the bar staff came out and told me there was a guy at the bar being a bit of a pest, I followed him back in, and he discreetly pointed him out to me, as usual he was bigger than me….much fucking bigger!

If I walked in and just knocked him out, I probably couldn't drag his body out afterwards, and I didn't fancy going toe to toe with him….so I watched him for a while.

I asked a couple of guys around the same age if they were his pals but nobody knew him; there was a group of two boys and two girls standing who he was trying to make conversation with, and one of the lads came over to me "Are you the fucking bouncer?" he asked….."I am mate" I replied….."Then do your fucking job and sort this cunt out will ya?" he growled……

Well I didn't like his tone at all…. "Yes I will"….I said…. "When I'm ready"……and he skulked off back to his little group.

The big guy had finished his drink, so I walked over and asked him to come to the front door for a chat. I often use this method, especially in nightclubs where its noisy and you have to shout. I say I want to speak to them at the front door where I can hear and speak properly, and when we get there I give them the good news that they're not going back in.

Anyway we get to the front door and he walks out, no bother at all, stands on the pavement and turns around, I'm on the step and he is still slightly taller than me!

"Let me back in" he says.

"Can't mate….your too pissed and your being a pest"

"Go on…..let me back in" he keeps saying; and then starts digging around in his pockets and offering me twenty pound notes to be allowed back in.

"Keep your money mate…go and get a kebab and go

home"……but would he fuck go away?

This went on for ages, and he was getting more and more irate, they were no police cars passing to move him on. I couldn't radio for the police as the radio was inside….at one point he tried to walk in and I shoved my hand against his chest….he just smirked and offered me another twenty quid!

"Look mate…you're on cctv, and pretty soon the police are going to come and move you on"……   well that was it…he fucking exploded…. "Fuck the police"…he started shouting "I'll kill the fucking lot of them"…he was ranting and raving…

"Well this is getting worse" I thought to myself, just then another lad from another venue turned up, he had come to collect something from the bar on his way to work…."Just hang on here a second" I tell him. So now there are two of us at the door; and this lad was quite chunky, I could see the big drunken fella thinking "Hmm….there's two of them now"….then he checked how much money he had left in his pocket and wandered off down the street…without saying another word.

The arsehole who had spoke to me inside earlier then came out (After big drunk guy had fucked off) and tried to get in my face…. "Why didn't you come in and knock that cunt out?" he says "I work the doors and that's not how we do it"

"Really?" I said….. "how old are you"

"Twenty one" he replied.

"Right….well I've done this job for longer than you've been alive mate….and if I had gone in and knocked him out, I've then got to drag the big lump out, no doubt on my own because despite being a doorman, you have kept your head down and out of the way the whole fucking time…..right up until the point that he fucked off….you didn't even have the balls to say anything when he was pestering your lass and her mate….where do you work the doors anyway?"

He mentioned some village that I had never heard of and can't remember; I looked at the other doorman and we both raised our eyebrows.

With that his girlfriend came out and they set off up the street, no doubt he was telling her how he told me how to do my job, and that it was lucky I took the guy outside when I did because he was just about to knock him out blah blah blah!

The Scene

The scene is the collective term for the area in Newcastle which contains its gay bars, historically known as the pink triangle, almost every bar in the area is a gay (or gay friendly) bar. Some newly built hotels have sprung up next to it and it is also next to one of the big concert venues; so it does get its fair share of straight custom as well.

The main night club Powerhouse is one of the only clubs in Newcastle which stays open until six a.m. at times, so that draws a lot of people in as well.

Like Mushroom, Perdu, and The Quilted Camel, one company owns a number of venues on the scene. If you work on one venue, it is often likely that you will at times work on another one of the seven venues owned by the group....rather than have a separate chapter for my time at each venue, I will just do them collectively as one.

Once again I was asked to do a bit of cover work, this time at Powerhouse by a guy who I had spoken to a couple of times at Cosy Joes, while working with his partner, and again, I ended up there for months.

My first night there was new years eve 2011 / 2012, and to be fair it was a bit of an eye opener. I had never been in a gay bar or club before, and I was a bit surprised. The atmosphere was much more relaxed than other nightclubs I had worked in, and there seemed to be much more energy amongst the crowd...but happy energy, people were getting on the stage and on the podiums and dancing;

but not dancing like the posers in the other clubs, who were practically doing photo shoots....these people were just going for it, really enjoying themselves...and not giving a fuck what anybody thought about them.

A lot of customers would ask if you had to be gay to be a doorman on a gay bar?....well, no you don't. I only know two gay doormen in Newcastle (there may be more...I don't know) one of them works down the scene, the other one used to (briefly) but now works in another nightclub in Newcastle, I have worked with them both. I used to attract quite a bit of attention when working down the scene, being a bit chunky with a smooth, freshly shaved head every night....guys (and girls) used to love stroking it....but once they know you're straight they tend to leave you alone, its all in good fun.

One night we were up in the VIP area at the end of the night after being paid, and one of the promo lads was waiting to go in the office for his wages. He was a large lad, very rotund, not the best looking, and he used to dress in some very outrageous outfits.

Anyway he says to me "Neil.....what's five times eight pound?"

"Forty quid mate" I replies.

"Right"...he says... "Forty quid...that's what I'll give you if you let me suck your cock"!....just like that...not a hint of embarrassment or anything...brazen as you like.

"Fuck off"....I laughed... "It's worth more than that"!

To be fair I was quite insulted; not that he had asked me, but because he thought it was only worthy of forty quid...

We always go to my mams on a Sunday for our tea, my daughters sometime come down with my granddaughter, and my sister, niece and her family also go along. I had told Donna about my proposal, which she found extremely amusing, she said I should have let him do it, as that would save her doing it?....My eldest daughter came in the kitchen where me and Donna are standing, and Donna says "Have you told Natalie about your proposition last night?"…well of course I had to tell her after that didn't I? Natalie found it thoroughly amusing, and went straight into the front room to tell all present….they said he mustn't have been expecting me to be very good if he was only offering forty quid…..bastards!

When on the door we would screen the queue; quite a few straight people were coming down as it was a bloody good club, but the locals knew it was gay friendly and what to expect, people from out of town on stag do's etc would turn up because people had said it was the best place to go to in Newcastle. Once we sussed they weren't locals we would let them know it was a gay friendly club and watch their reaction, if there was any indication at all they were homophobic then they weren't getting in….even if it was in jest on their behalf, they didn't get in.

One part of the club which attracted a particular crowd was a room called the purple room….by a particular crowd I mean a shit crowd. It was dark, mainly lit by neon lights, and played hardcore rave music. It was a shit magnet but apparently it took a lot of money, so we had to put up with it.

The main club area was on the first floor, then the purple room was on the second floor along with access to the stairs for the smoking terrace and toilets, and the VIP area and offices were on the third floor.

As it was only a small room it only warranted one door supervisor, and the ones who were floating would pop in as they were wandering about. Every time there was a shout from the purple room I would run in and trip on the raised dance floor! It was always pitch black, and I'm sure the DJ used to point the smoke machine at the door and set it off when he knew we were coming. Two or three times I actually tumbled across the floor running in, and a number of times I would reach out when I tripped and customers would grab me and hold me up!

One time when it kicked off in there I went running up the stairs, and the guys had somebody out of the room and on the landing by the time I got there, but there were still two flights of stairs to go down. Anyway the guy is struggling, and as usual his lovely girlfriend is shouting and screaming at the door staff and trying to pull them off her boyfriend. He calms down a bit and they get him down the first flight of stairs, I'm looking on and keeping the stairs clear so they can get him down without knocking anybody over, at the top of the next (and final) flight of stairs he kicks off.

The lads are restraining him and then all of a sudden he breaks free and throws himself down the stairs…lying unconscious at the bottom…."Fuck me" I thought "This looks nasty".

We go to the bottom of the stairs and one of the lads starts dragging him up off the floor "Fuck him"..he says "I've seen him do this before, pretends he takes fits and everything this one".

And with that the guy suddenly goes berserk again, lashing out at everybody, whereby the fire exit door is swiftly kicked open and he is thrown out onto the pavement. He is only yards from the door once out the fire exit, and has had an amazing recovery, he is now definitely full of beans and wants to fight the lot of us, at one point he tried to pick a bin up off the pavement to throw at us, but it was bolted down so he couldn't. We all thought that was hilarious, but it just made him more annoyed.

We went out to him and kept him away from the door so people could still get in and out, at one point I stepped forward and offered him my chin (silly I know, but we were starting to get bored), "Go on" I said..pointing at my chin "You can have the first shot….put one on there"

He looked at me and was probably thinking "Who's this fucking lunatic?" but wouldn't make a move…

"Either kick off or fuck off….ya fucking dickhead" I said….he kept huffing and puffing but was backing further down the street as time went on, eventually he fucked off and went to the pizza shop next door. It wasn't long before he was annoying people in there and ended up fighting outside, but that's nothing to do with us!

From experience I would say the main trouble inside the venues down there was from females, we would have a fair bit of confrontation at the front door from males that had been knocked back, but the girls were the fighters inside.

One night a group of girls were fighting on the stairs, they had been arguing upstairs about somebody looking at somebody funny or something stupid like that, when the door staff started walking them out.

Part way down the stairs it kicks off and we get the shout to go in, we got to them and started pulling them apart. I'm taking a blonde girl down the stairs and leaning against the handrail so I can keep my balance; when I feel thump, thump, thump, on the top of my head. I look up and this bird is leaning over the handrail of the stairs above, bashing me in the fucking head with her handbag!....I didn't want to bash her properly so I reached through the spindles of the stairs above and pushed her knee sideways....she stumbled in her porn star heels and fell on her arse, bless her.

We got downstairs and held the blonde girl in the cloakroom (it turned out she was the one the rest wanted to beat up). The others got slung out the front door. After we had cleaned the blonde girl up a bit we let her out the back door of the club. A few minutes later somebody ran to the front saying there was a fight at the back door, the girls had somehow spotted the blonde girl and set upon her at the back of the club....we started pulling them apart, there were high heels, handbags and hair extensions flying everywhere, the girls were fucking wild....worse than men!

A womans adrenaline release is slower than a mans, so while a man gets a sudden rush and wants to kick off, but then starts to calm down, a womans takes longer to reach its peak....so while the guys are calming down, the girls are just fucking getting going!

Anyway, we pulled them all apart, and I think the police collared a few of them, with me being the first aider I was left to see to the blonde girl until the ambulance got there. She was in a right mess. Clumps of her hair had been pulled out and her head was bleeding, a couple of her fingernails (real, not false) had come off, her mouth was in a right mess; she was starting to struggle speaking because of the damage to her lips and tongue…but she was looking on the ground for something?

She was looking for her teeth….they had kicked two of her teeth out; and she wanted to find them so she could try and get them put back in!

Wandering around the club one night I came across a couple having an argument, nothing special but they were being a bit loud, she was, anyway. He was a big fella; his t shirt was probably a size too small for him as it was tight as fuck, and cut at the neck to show off what he probably thought were decent pecs. She was in a short, tight, sleeveless dress which showed off all of her tattoos, and monster porn star heels!….she was a classy bird, all of her tattoos were spelt right, even the ones on her knuckles!

"Guys" I say to them "Keep it down or you will have to go…yeah?"

"Yeah, Yeah mate" he says….and I know full well they aren't gonna stop…you just know.

After a few minutes they are still going at it, and she is getting louder and louder, I go over and say "Come on guys…can you sort this out downstairs?"

"Yeah mate, we're going" he says, and he walks out and down the stairs, with her stamping after him.

Of course once they get outside it all starts again doesn't it? She picks up from where she left off and is really going for it….screaming and swearing at him!

He has got his hands out in front of him trying to calm her down when WHOOSH!…she swings her handbag round in a big arc and clumps him right on the ear with it….knocking him clean out.

Now it's not funny, the poor guy is lying flat out on the pavement, but we can't help but have a little snigger….but then the momentum of her bag swinging pulls her round with it, she spins round, breaking a heel as she goes, and topples over onto her arse next to him, legs in the air and flashing her knickers to everyone. Well that was it, we were doubled over laughing, even the usual nurses and army medics didn't come forward to help as they were all having a good laugh.

She sorts herself out just as he is coming round, she looks in her bag and then off she goes again…shouting and swearing at him. He just got up and fucked off, shaking his head at her. There was a big wet patch on the ground where she had fallen, we thought she had pissed herself but it wasn't, it was from the big bottle of vodka she had in her bag smashing when she fell over….no wonder it knocked him out!….and she was blaming him for it getting smashed!

We were always kept on our toes on the front door of Powerhouse, as it was always nice and steady with people coming in, going out, falling over etc. There were three or four us on the door on a weekend, and three of us were standing chatting outside one night when something flew past our faces.

"What the fuck was that?" I asked, and looked to my right just in time to see a woman in a black dress throw the other shoe.

The shoe missed me and was heading for Paul (not his real name). It was one of the chunky black ones with spiky studs sticking out the full length of the stiletto heel…I was fucking glad it missed me!

Paul turned and ducked at the same time. The shoe hit him on the back of the shoulder and landed on the pavement.

The woman is now standing shoeless about thirty feet

away; shouting and swearing at us, calling us all kind of names. I had never even seen her before?

"Who's she?" I asked.

"Just some daft lass we knocked back earlier" he replied.

"Do you want these back….do you….you fucking nutter?" he was shouting at her now, holding both shoes by the heels above his head

"Give me them back now ya bastard" she screamed (lovely girl).

"Go and fucking get them" Paul shouts; and with that he turns and throws her shoes into the middle of the dual carriageway that runs alongside the gable end of the club.

Immature I know….but we had a good laugh watching her trying to get them back.

Next door to Powerhouse is a bar called Gossip.

On a weekend there will be one doorman on gossip who is linked via radio to the door staff at Powerhouse; the two doors are roughly ten to fifteen metres apart.

We had a new guy on Gossip one night, and to be fair he wasn't very good…big lump of a guy, buy no good at the job.

At one point of the night he shouts because some girls are fighting in the bar and we run over to give him a hand. We get in there and the fight has stopped, but he points out the two girls who were fighting with one other girl. Now these two didn't look like fighters; they were proper pretty little things, one blond and one brunette, anyway they are asked to leave and they walk out….no dramas.

A little while later he shouts again, we run over and into the bar, where there is a commotion in the seating booths to the right of the dance floor. He is standing in the middle of the dance floor pointing us in the direction of the bother…doing fuck all?

I can see its two girls who have another person pinned down on the seats….and they are going for it. We run over and start grabbing bodies and hair and pulling these two off whoever is underneath….we throw them off and I turn back to the person lying on the seats.

She's unconscious, so I drag her on the floor and start going through my first aid….can she hear me?...no response…is she breathing?....

As I'm leaning over her checking her breathing she starts fitting, and not a little fit, a proper thrashing around fit….shoes coming off and everything!

We quickly move the stools and tables out of the way and let her get on with it. She stops fitting so I put her in the recovery position. I like to half lean over people in this situation with the backs of my fingers up to their nose and mouth so I can feel any breathing, and with my hand on their back so I can feel the body moving as they breath. By only half leaning over I can also watch what is going on around me, as a couple of times I have had people try to kick me or throw things at me whilst giving first aid!

After about thirty seconds she started fitting again, another nasty one. A friend of hers had appeared and I asked if her pal was epileptic; and if she took any medication….her friend said she didn't think she was epileptic, and she had known her for years.

She stopped fitting again, so again I put her in the recovery position as I had before, and I was thinking "I hope this fucking ambulance hurries up"

Then she stopped breathing.

"Fucks sake" I thought "Why me?"…which was a bit selfish seeing it was her who was in a mess, not me. I rolled her on her back and got ready to perform CPR……..

Just as I bent over to start giving her chest compressions she coughed and spluttered a bit…"Thank fuck for that" I thought.

Well then the paramedics arrived and we went through what happened etc and they took her away. The police came back later for the cctv footage and to have a chat with us, it turns out the girl wasn't epileptic, but one of the attackers had been hitting her on the head with a stiletto heel, which may have dented the skull and affected the poor girls brain….resulting in her taking the fits.

Over the 2012 / 2013 Christmas period I worked down the scene, I worked every night except Christmas day night. On the Christmas eve I didn't get back in the house until after four in the morning, I got in and the kids' presents were all laid out, "they'll be up in a couple of hours" I thought it was pointless going to bed, so I slept on the floor for a couple of hours with our dogs. Everybody got up and we opened our presents, but by ten o clock I was knackered and starting to get a bit ratty, so I put myself to bed for a bit before dinner.
This is the kind of impact the job can have on your life, especially if you have family. You don't see them at night because you are at work, and then you lose time with them the next day as you are in bed sleeping, yes we choose to do it, but some do it out of necessity, and their family life and relationships can suffer because of it.
Luckily I have a wife who doesn't put any pressure on me in that respect, to be fair she is glad when I am out of the house and at work on the doors, it means she has the bed to herself and can get to sleep without my snoring keeping her awake. Down side for me is I have to go home and try to get to sleep with her snoring next to me….keeping me awake!
Anyway….I digress.

That Christmas eve I was working at Rusty's. I had never worked at Rusty's before and I was going to be on my own until around one o clock, when one of lads from another bar was going to come and finish the shift with me. I'm not a lover of one man doors, but they weren't expecting it to be busy, and I could call on the lads from the other bars if need be.
I'm standing in the doorway of the bar, with my right hand

on the door handle, looking inside through the glass panels, but keeping an eye out for approaching customers from my left so I can open the door for them.

Out of the corner of my eye I notice somebody approaching, red high heels, black fishnets, nice legs, and a very, very short, tight Santa clause outfit…. "This looks alright" I think to myself as I start to open the door and turn to look at the approaching goddess.

"Alright mate?.....I'm Adam" says the sexy Santa clause!

"Hello mate"….I replied, a little bit stunned "You having a good night?" I asked.

"Not too bad kidda" …. He said, shaking my hand "Fucking freezing with this dress on though!"

When the other lad came down at one o clock I was telling him about my sexy Santa.

"Oh that's Adam"….. he says "He's a regular….only got one bollock you know?"

Apparently Adam had one of his testicles bitten off by a woman; who was giving him a blow job in the pub toilets, whilst Adam was dressed as a woman?

One night over the Christmas period I was working at Switch, the bar next door was called The Bank (as it was a converted bank), and the two were joined together by a room upstairs.

I'm standing on the door and two of my pals turned up, we were standing chatting when two of (one of) my sons teachers came up to the door, I have three sons aged sixteen, fifteen and nine (at time of writing), the fifteen year old was a bit of a handful in high school, and I had been to see Mr D his pastoral head a number of times regarding his behaviour. Whenever I went to see him I was always smartly dressed and polite, I don't know if he knew what I did for a living, but I'm sure he knew I was self employed and worked in security.

Anyway two of his teachers turn up, one of whom used to

regularly come into Switch and Powerhouse, we are standing shaking hands and one of them tells me that Mr D (my sons pastoral head) is out with them, and points over my shoulder.

I turn around and there's Mr D, who is quite a bit worse for wear and a bit wobbly, I have just shook his hand when one of my pals who I had been chatting to tapped me on the shoulder.

"Look at him" he said, and I turned to see my other pal wrestling with some kid. He has the kid in a headlock and is trying to punch him in the head.

Forgetting about Mr D I run over and get stuck into the pair of them, trying to pull them apart. I separate them and push my pal my pal out of the way, and then the other kid turns on me, throwing silly wild punches. I grab him and take him to the ground, choking him to slow him down a bit and put him off fighting me, and I'm a bit annoyed by now so I'm doing a bit of swearing as well.

Mr D was probably thinking "Fuck me….no wonder the sons a bit of a shit if that's his role model!"

I spent New Years Eve 2012 / 2013 working at Switch, and at midnight I was stood outside on my own, listening to the customers counting down and celebrating the arrival of the new year….I had a little sigh to myself and thought "I wonder where I will be this time next year?"

Legends / The Den

Legends nightclub was situated underground, opposite Newcastle's main theatre, it had been there as long as I could remember, I used to drink in there back in 1987. It had evolved from a bright; glitzy nightclub into a dark, gloomy venue catering for the rock and alternative crowd, however it did also hold student nights....I much preferred the alternative / rock crowd to the students!
Unfortunately, at time of writing Legends recently closed, and is apparently going to re open as a restaurant.

After working the Christmas and New Year period I decided to have a little break from the doors, the bars normally go quiet in the New Year, and door numbers get cut, so I knew I wouldn't be missed.

A pal of mine got in touch with me and asked if I wanted a shift working a night called "Clash of The Titans" in Legends, the night was on once a month and the door team was always increased for it....I accepted to work that cover shift....and ended up working there eight months!

Clash of the titans was an event where a lot of MC's would come together in the club and take turns doing their thing on the stage. Basically they would shout / talk shit very loudly into their microphones, personally I thought they were all shit, they all sounded the same, the beat of the music was the same all fucking night, and I couldn't understand a word any of them said, and the crowd they attracted was all the shit from the shit areas….in summary it was a shit night, and the door staff dreaded it coming round every month!

We arrived at nine o clock and I was asked to work the stage, I would stand at one side of the stage and if anybody except an MC got on the stage, I was to get them off….easy peasy. I stood by the stage for six hours, and in all that time I only had to get people off it three times, and two of those times it was the same person….the second time I advised him that if he kept taking the piss and getting on the stage, then he would be thrown out. After paying twenty pound to get in; I don't think he fancied getting slung out, and he never got back on the stage….but he did give me a thumbs up every time I caught his eye after that…bless him.

The night went without incident, and I was thinking "What are these all moaning about….apart from the shit music and shit people…the nights not too bad?"

The regular team at Legends at that time was myself, Mick (head doorman), Marc and Gary. Mick and Gary were normally upstairs and Me, Marc, and any extra guys who were working would be downstairs.

When I first started there, and for the first few weeks, I wondered if Mick actually had any hands. Mick would stand at the front door; in his big parka coat, with his hands in his coat pockets….every time I went upstairs his hands were in his pockets.

We were working on one of the clash of the titans nights, and Me, Mick and Gary were on the front door. Gary and I were stood at either side of the entrance doors, and Mick was stood between us, just to my right.

Mick had knocked some guy back for being too pissed,

and the guy was protesting, saying Mick had to let him in as he was an MC, and was due to perform….we knew he wasn't, so we kept telling him to politely go away.

The guy prowled around outside for a bit; moaning and groaning and calling us names, when all of a sudden he came striding towards the door.

We stepped forward as one, shoulder to shoulder, forming a "wall of doormen". MC Fuckwit got the message, realized he wasn't gonna get past us and fucked off….Mick stood in the middle, grinning, cool as fuck, and with his hands still in his pockets!

Another Saturday night I was working downstairs with Marc, and something kicked off on the dance floor. I ran over and dragged some kid in a black top off another. He was in a sitting position on the floor, with his back to me, so I got him in a rear choke and leant on him… "Fucking calm down son… I'm a doorman" I shouted in his ear. He put his arms out to the side and relaxed. I got him up and we walked out to the front door.

Whilst at the front door a couple of his pals came up and a bit of an argument ensued. The four of us were upstairs by then, Me, Mick and Gary in our usual formation, with Marc stood just behind us.

Anyway the kid in the black top and his pal got excited, and Mr black top took a swing at Mick….and then it happened….they appeared!

Mick's hands left his pockets and grabbed Mr black top, wrapping him up and putting him on the ground, I was busy with his pal, and both me and Mick ended up on the ground, with our opponents pinned face down, noses squashed against the pavement.

Mick had a little word in his new mates ear, and convinced the guy it was in his best interest to just fuck off…which they did.

We got up and went to the door, I sorted myself out and then looked over to Mick who was back in his usual spot, cool as fuck, grinning, and of course…..with his hands in his pockets!

People say you should count to ten when somebody or something is annoying you, well Marc used to count to eight, we used to call it "The eight second rule".

If somebody was in Marc's face, they would have eight seconds to fuck off, once they eight seconds was up then you would feel the back of his right hand, sharply striking you on the head somewhere.

At one point Marc broke his right hand, but was still coming to work with his cast on, so obviously he couldn't apply the eight second rule for fear of either further damaging his hand, or giving somebody a nasty bruise from his plaster cast.

We were clearing the club at the end of the night, and some guy was being a bit of a knob with Marc, and getting in his face….. "Hmmm"….I thought "What will happen here?... and started counting.

I had almost reached eight, when Marc switched his stance and hit the guy with an almighty back hander, but with his left hand this time. It rocked the guy, and I then went over to walk him out. We all went upstairs together and the guy was escorted outside.

The guy wasn't impressed that he had been clipped, but Marc was very impressed with himself that he had managed to land such a cracking shot with his less dominant hand!

I experienced my first "stand off" at Legends, and guess what?....it was at a clash of the titans night!

It had been a pretty quiet night as there wasn't many in, the attendance figures for these nights were getting less and less and each month.

I had been working upstairs on the front door, but had gone downstairs for a bit. It was after two o clock, and I had spotted somebody asleep in one of the seating areas. I woke him up and was walking him out when one of the glass collecting staff ran up to me and said there was a fight on the dance floor.

I left my new sleepy friend and ran around to the dance floor, I saw the commotion, and when I focused on it I noticed a group of about four or five lads were bearing down on one lone lad, throwing punches at him. Training tells us to do a dynamic risk assessment as we are approaching a situation, assess the situation and decide if you can handle it yourself; or if you need to, to call it in and wait for help….well I just ran straight into the middle of it!

The guy on his own was on his back foot, so I ran in so I was facing him, between him and his attackers. I ran him backwards away from them, and got a couple of punches in the back of the head for my trouble. I left the four of five attackers for the other door lads to sort out.

Then there was a shout on the radio "All door staff to dance floor….all door staff to dance floor". Now there would have been about ten or twelve door staff on that night, so if they are shouting for all door staff to attend, it must be pretty bad. When it goes off you don't think; you just react, I left the guy I had just rescued leaning against the bar and ran around the dance floor….

The dance floor had cleared, anybody dancing had moved up towards the stage at one end, and I could see about ten doormen lined up at the other end. I pushed into the line so I was about third from the left; and then I saw what we were facing.

There was twelve of them; they had came in three taxis, and just walked straight in past the two door lads who were upstairs, without paying….straight in and straight downstairs. This wasn't a reflection on the lads upstairs, as quite often the promoter would arrange for kids to get in for free etc.

They had came with the sole purpose of finding that one lad….and punching his face in, once he was spotted they went for it, and now here we were!

These kids were all tasty fighters, and I remember thinking "If this kicks off we are fucked", I knew a few of the lads working could have a scrap and hold their own, but I had my doubts about at least four of them. It was a tense time. I was still pretty new to the venue so was following the lead of the regular guys. I was a bit puzzled as to why we were having this stand off, and nobody was throwing anybody out, fighting, or even talking, but I thought "When they get stuck in, I'll get stuck in"

This stand off seemed to last for ages, but it was probably less than a minute or two….the music had stopped and the lights had come on….there was no noise, but that could have been the adrenaline blocking that out.

I heard footsteps coming down the stairs and into the club, then saw the yellow hi vis police vests. Once the police appeared the attackers and their pals dispersed without a word, and the police let them go quietly.

At the end of the night a few of the regular lads were chatting about it, we all agreed how naughty that could have turned out, and how lucky we all were to come out of it unscathed. After that incident we implemented (via the manager) a rule whereby nobody was allowed access to the club after two o clock, unless they had been in earlier, and had a stamp to prove it.

At another one of these nights there had been a couple of people complaining about a lad going round threatening people, trying to start fights outside in the smoking area etc.

I went downstairs with one guy who had complained, and he pointed the instigator out, he was on the dance floor. I walked over and asked him to come upstairs to the front door where I could talk to him…pointing at my ear and saying that it was too loud to talk to him there.

He came up to the front door and we told him he wasn't

going back in, before he could reply a guy he had been threatening downstairs started getting in his face, they were having a bit of an argument, pushing and shoving, when a guy next to me said to his pal…"That's the kid who punched me downstairs". So then his pal got stuck in.

We were standing back watching all of this going on…it was now out in the street after all, the cctv would pick it up and the police would attend.

Anyway his pal runs over and grabs the instigator, pinning him against a van which was parked outside the club. They have a bit of a cuddle and then he pushes him off, hitting him with a well timed left, right combination from a classic boxers stance, knocking the instigator clean out…he is lying unconscious on his back, In the crucifix position. Then the puncher walks over and stamps on the instigators head….naughty.

Another kid runs over and pushes the puncher away from the instigator, then the original guy runs over and hits him with a sucker punch…knocking him out!

It's all getting a bit messy now, two lads are on the floor unconscious, the instigator is bleeding from his ear, where part of it was bitten off when he was pinned against the van. Girls are screaming and crying, little groups of pals are trying to get involved and are having little scuffles….we are just standing watching, not phased at all. As I said earlier you become desensitized to the violence, we had seen it all before.

The police turned up and the two punchers did a runner down the street, one of their cars was actually parked outside and they jumped in that and drove off.

The instigator got up and wandered off, I believe to the police station and then the hospital….the police came back a couple of times looking for the piece of his ear which was now missing, but I don't think they ever found it.

I'm standing outside one Saturday night, and Marc brings these two Russian guys up and out the front door….they were your classic jeans / biker jacket kind of rockers, with their long hair and baseball caps, and noisy fucking arseholes to boot!

I had noticed them a few weeks ago inside, and tonight they were dicking about....so Marc had shown them the door.

Anyway, a few weeks pass, and these two Russians turn up in the queue on a Saturday night.

One of them wandered off to the shop around the corner, so I had a wander down the queue to give his mate the good news..... "Sorry bud...but you're not coming in here tonight" I tell him.

"Why not?" He asks, in a Russian accent, obviously.

"Cos you were thrown out a few weeks ago, so you're not coming back in.....sorry"

"Not me" he replies...... "I was in Russia two weeks ago"

Here we go, I thought, and had a little sigh to myself........ "listen mate....there are only two Russians, who dress like you, who come in here....and it's you and your mate....you're not coming in, so move out the queue and go somewhere else"

I stood side on as he moved out of the queue.....I then turned and walked back to the door.

Anyway....his mate returns from the shop and they have a little chat....no doubt reaching the conclusion that I'm a dickhead!....and they stride up the path towards me.

"Why can't we come in?".....shouts his pal....(With a Russian accent)

"I've already told your mate"....I replied "Ask him....he will tell you on your way to the next bar".

"Well I'm asking YOU!" he shouts, and he pokes me in the chest.....and I hate being poked in the chest!

I knew now he was gonna get a smack, and I was already stood on an angle in front of him, with my left hand up at chest height and my right hand down by my side....I was looking for the pre emptive strike.

There was only me and Gary on the door, and I knew he

would have stopped the queue by now and be waiting to see how this panned out.....

"Don't fucking poke me mate.....There's no need for that"

"Is that right"?....he says (poke)....."I'll poke you if I fucking want to".... He says (poke)

That was it, there was the trigger, BANG.....my right hand came up from down by my side and slammed into the side of his jaw....just below the ear....smack on the button.

Over he went, and landed on his arse, accompanied by a chorus of cheers and "Oooh's" from the people in the queue....his mate ran towards me screaming "You crazy man"!

I turned to face him and really turned it on, hoping to put him off actually having a go.... "Do you fucking want some?" I shouts....which stopped him in his tracks.

Gary jumps in between us and does his referee impersonation....legs apart and both hands sticking out....keeping us away from each other.

Just then a police car pulls up and bundles the Russians in.....the whole thing had been being watched by the local cctv.

They were promptly taken away.....and to this day they never came back to the club!

The next day I was looking through Facebook and Youtube expecting to see a video of the knockout, accompanied by lots of comments about how nasty us doormen are, and how we always go over the top etc. It's all too common now, and people will whip their mobile phones out and video the situation when they see one developing. I have been present when people have been ejected; and then began antagonizing the door staff, trying to actually get hit, and they have told their mates to film it for evidence.

I've been caught with two sucker punches in my "career".....the first was mentioned earlier, in Tynemouth, the second was at legends!

It was a few weeks after the incident with the Russians, on a quiet Friday night, and I was in my usual spot on the door upstairs. I was getting a bit bored; so I went downstairs for a look around; and noticed a young guy standing against the barrier around the edge of the dance floor, asleep. I gave him a little shake and he came round a little..."Come on buddy....let's go upstairs for a bit fresh air" I said, and with that me and Tony led him upstairs.

Once upstairs and outside, true to form he started kicking off.....demanding to go back in and get his girlfriend, which he was advised was not going to happen. Anyway; we had a little wrestle, and he had to be restrained until he calmed down. Once he saw he wasn't getting anywhere he calmed down, and stood on the opposite side of the door from me, behind Gary.

Tony had gone in to find his girlfriend, who obviously wasn't fucking bothered that he had been thrown out because she was still in there, and I could see them heading up the stairs. I leant towards him and said "Here, your girlfriend is coming now"....and looked down the stairs towards her.

Bang!.....he punched me right in the mouth as I was looking down the stairs....I sort of heard it more than felt it, and straight away he tried to do a runner...

I managed to grab his shirt sleeve and pull him down to the ground, I got on top and pinned him down by the throat with my right hand, and got three good digs in with my left....breaking his nose....his girlfriend then joined the party and kicked me in the face with her converse. Tony was on my back trying to pull me off one way; his girlfriend was trying to pull me off the other way, and the usual crowd of passersby had formed and were sticking their noses in....shouting about the nasty doorman assaulting the poor helpless boy who was bleeding on the ground....and of course there were a few arseholes running round shouting they were a nurse or an army medic!

I didn't care who was trying to pull me off, I just wanted

to cause as much damage to him as I could.

Anyway; Tony dragged me off him and I go back inside the door to sort my top lip out, which the little twat had split open.

After cleaning myself up I go back outside, and the cheeky fucker has only came back to the door and is apologizing to Gary for causing trouble, and asking why can't he come back in the club....by then I couldn't be bothered to roll around the floor again, so he was told to fuck off and not come back....got to admire him for coming back though!

My lip took days to heal, I couldn't shave properly, and every time I smiled or laughed it would open up and start bleeding again, ...who knows, maybe it was karma biting me on the arse for knocking the Russian out!

The guys brought a lad out one night and he was only wearing one shoe!...apparently his shoe had come off as he was getting dragged out and he wanted it back.

He had been left outside with and the lads had gone back inside, we were having the usual "Why was he thrown out / I didn't know why, I didn't throw him out conversation", when he started demanding I let him go back in to find his shoe. To be fair his shoes were a bit shit anyway (the one he was still wearing!), scruffy, flimsy white things that were falling to bits.

Any way he is going on, and on, and on about this shoe, and I am trying to be patient and tell him he can't go back in for it tonight, but if he comes back on Monday night he can get it from reception....and then he starts shouting.

"Let me go and get my Fucki".....SLAP.

His shoe flew through the air and bounced off the side of his face, spinning up into the air, cutting his rant short. One of the lads had been downstairs for it so we could get rid of him.

I couldn't help but burst out laughing which seemed to enrage him even more, he lunged at me but I just grabbed him, put him on the ground and tied his arms up, restraining him.

"Whoa…whoa, bonny lad…..calm yourself down man, you've got your shoe back, so just fuck off somewhere else…come back another time" I said…still giggling.

He relaxed a bit and (I think) saw the funny side of it, but after all of the palaver about getting his shoe back he didn't even put it on…he picked it up and walked away carrying it!

My most recent run in with the police occurred at Legends, on a Saturday night.

Kev had brought this lad out for some reason, and once thrown out he was hanging around outside the club, having a moan to anyone who would listen to him, to look at he wasn't much of a threat, a little bit taller than me, skinny, with lank curly hair.

He came up to me on the door and demanded to be told why he had been thrown out.

"Don't know mate….I didn't throw you out" I replied.

"Let me back in then" he demanded.

"No".

And he wandered off….but not far; he was still close enough so I could hear him moaning to people about being thrown out for nothing.

Then he came back…a little more agitated this time.

"I want my cigarettes" he shouts.

"Well I haven't got them mate?" I replied….he started bouncing around on his toes, getting a bit more agitated.

"Then go in there and fucking get them"…he shouts, "I want them now!"

"Don't be stupid mate….just fuck off" I told him.

He came back to the door a couple of more times, (seven times in total) each time he was more agitated than the last, he was demanding to see the doorman who had threw him out, he wanted to see our licenses, he wanted our badge numbers, he wanted to see the manager to put a complaint in about the door staff, he then went away from the door and was stopping people as they were approaching the club and telling them that were cunts, and to tell us that we were cunts on their way in.

People were coming in the club and saying "That guy up there says to tell you that you're a cunt".

There was a bit of a commotion down the street at this point; and some dickheads were pulling wheelie bins over onto the road, I could see where my car was parked from the door, and some of the bins looked pretty close to them, so I had a wander down to check.

On the way back up I could see something going on at the door of the club; the guy Kev had thrown out was lying on his back a few yards down from the door, and Kev was standing over him (the guy had came to the door and went for Kev, so Kev had put him on his arse and then dragged him by the ankle away from the door).

As I approached, Kev had turned and was walking away from him, and he was getting to his feet and making a bee line for Kevs back.

I ran up behind him and grabbed his t shirt, pulling him back, as he turned to face me I could see he wasn't in the mood for a chat, so I grabbed him by the throat with both hands and started to choke him; there were some wooden construction fence boards up around the building next door, and I pinned him against them, pressing his face into them.

"Calm the fuck down" I was shouting at him….but he was still struggling, somebody grabbed me and was saying "Mr Bouncer, Mr Bouncer…you're strangling him"…..I knew what I was doing, I didn't need anybody to tell me?

A couple of people were now trying to pull us apart (as they do), I still had him bent over, gripping his throat, my fingers were applying pressure to his carotid arteries, not his windpipe….the idea is to slow down or interrupt the blood flow to the brain, either to slow them down or if need be render them unconscious.

I dragged him along the hoardings a little bit, and then let him go. As I let him go he sort of half stumbled a couple of steps and fell to the ground. When he got back up he had a pretty decent cut over his eye, there was no blood on the hoardings, so it must have happened when he fell.

Oddly enough he didn't come back to the door again that night (cheeky fucker tried to get in a few weeks later, and started demanding to see licenses etc again when we knocked him back). A few of his mates starting fussing around him and called him an ambulance.

Then we got a visit from the police.

The police came and asked for the cctv footage of the incident; the only coverage was of the times when he kept returning to the door, none of the carry on against the hoardings was captured.

Kev and I were both asked to go in and make statements, which we did. When I went in the police officer asked me how long I had been a doorman? What I did during the day?

I told her I was a trainer and that I delivered the governing body training courses to door staff, and that I also taught the approved physical intervention techniques.

She asked how we were taught to handle confrontation, and I took her through the conflict management techniques, non aggressive stance and trying to calm the customer down etc.

I explained that early in the incident when he wasn't being so aggressive, cctv showed our stance and mannerisms to be quite relaxed, as he wasn't really threatening at that point, however as time went on, it was evident from the cctv images of our positioning and stance that he was becoming more aggressive....our behaviour was reflecting his level of aggression.

I then went through the story of how I saw him go after Kev, I had restrained him against the hoardings, let him go, and he fell over.

We were both fingerprinted, photographed, and interviewed under caution.

I saw the police officer a couple of times after the incident, and I would ask her if there was any progress with the situation. Every time she would just say "I wouldn't worry about it"....in the end I just stopped asking, and nothing more came of it.

Just like at Sunderland Dogs; there was no letter confirming "No further action", no phone call....nothing, it just went away!

A member of bar staff came up to the front door one night and told us a girl had passed out in the toilets. This wasn't unusual, they would just get so drunk they would pass out, but we had to be mindful that it could be because they had suffered a seizure, or taken some bad drugs, I have been on the ladies toilet floor many times trying to bring unconscious girls round. Quite often when doing toilet checks at the end of the night we would find girls who had went to the toilet, fell asleep, and just been left in the club by their mates.

Two of us went into the toilets, and took a female member of bar staff in with us as well, as a witness. The girls don't bat an eyelid when door staff go into the toilets, they just carry on with whatever they are doing. There was an empty cubicle next to the one that this girl was in, so I went in and climbed on the toilet seat so I could see over the top....it wasn't pretty.

She had passed out and slid onto the floor, where she was curled up against the door. She had a dress on, and her underwear was around her ankles. She was a big girl, and I mean big...from what I could see she had also vomited on herself, this was getting better all the time....we couldn't open the door, she was covered in vomit and lying in the piss and beer on the floor! At least she was breathing, I knew this cos I could hear her snoring!

I couldn't climb over, so Bob (not his real name) started banging on the door, trying to wake her. He suggested throwing cold water over her but I didn't think that was a good idea. After much banging and shouting from us, and even louder snoring from her, we decided we couldn't wake her to unlock the door, so we decided to kick it in. It didn't take much to kick the locking mechanism off the frame, but because she was lying against the door it didn't exactly fly open, we then had to push and shove against the door to slide her along the floor, far enough so we could open the door and get in the cubicle.

As we were shoving against the door she came round, and didn't have a clue where she was. She turned and sat against the toilet (still on the floor); with her legs bent as if she was giving birth!

"Pull your knickers up pet" I said….as it wasn't a pretty sight.

We couldn't get any sense out of her, and she wasn't responding when we were telling her to stand up. I looked at Bob, and Bob looked at me.

"You'll have to pick her up" I said to him….

"Fuck off"….he replied "You pick her up"

We stood arguing for a little while about who was going to pick her up, meanwhile the classy bird on the floor covered in vomit and piss was sick on herself again. That was it for Bob, he started gagging and fucked off out of the toilets, leaving me and the barmaid in the toilets with her…. I looked at the barmaid "I'm not touching her" she said, shaking her head.

I sighed and reached down for her hand…. "Come on….stand up" I shouted, pulling on her arm….nothing. "Fucking hell she's heavy" I thought to myself, and reached down for the other hand… "Come on pet…make an effort…on three….one….two" I braced myself… "Three"…and I pulled.

As I pulled she stood up, but she didn't stand up and then stay stood up, she stood up and fell against me, covering my jacket in her vomit….and the smell was horrendous. Once on her feet and steadied she wasn't too bad, and I managed to walk her out of the toilets and to the stairs pretty easily.

At the stairs we had a bit of a mission, trying to get her to hold the banister and pull herself up while I am trying to support her and not get any more vomit or piss on me. I was looking up the stairs and the rest of the lads were standing laughing and taking the piss; I was shouting for them to give me a hand but none of them would…bastatrds! They all just found the whole thing very amusing.

Eventually I got her upstairs to the front door, and we called the street pastors to come and get her, because there was no way a taxi would take her. They would look after her until she could sort out getting home somehow.

There was still an hour or so of the night to go, I took my jacket off for the rest of the night but I was still stinking. I spent the rest of the night cold, on the front door, getting funny looks off customers who must have been wondering what the smell was.

Sometimes when I was at Legends I would work at a bar called The Den on a Friday, which was primarily a student crowd. I would be on the back door with someone else, which mainly served as the smoking area. It was generally always busy at the back door; and your time was spent moving people away from the door, checking stamps etc.

A guy came out the back door and was standing having a smoke amongst the crowd, he finished his cigarette and then started joining in a conversation with a couple of girls, being a bit sleazy and insulting one of them. They couldn't be bothered with him and told him to piss off; which alerted a boyfriend of theirs, who then started having a little scuffle with him.

Anyway he tried to come back in the club and I told him he couldn't come back in; when asked why, I didn't want to say "Because I think you're a dick"…I just said "I just don't want you back in….you look like you are intent on causing trouble".

He then started slagging me off; calling me all sorts of names, asking if I did the job because I couldn't do anything else? did it make me feel big? was it because I had a small knob? Etc

"Listen mate…you best just fuck off before you get clipped" I said to him…I was in my "Thinkers stance" as I didn't know what to expect from him, he was coming across as just a bit of a shouter, but the more they go on and build themselves up, the more likely they are to have a go and kick off.

"My coats inside….I need to go and get my coat" he shouts.

"Tough shit mate…you should have thought of that". I didn't believe him anyway, I had heard that one many times before.

"You can't stop me going in there" he stated….he was now starting to get interesting.

"Really?....you just try and go in then…see what fucking happens son" I replied…looking him right in the eye.

"You can't touch me"….he shouts "That would be assault…you can't come anywhere near me…you can't cross that line"….he was gesturing at some line on the ground, I didn't have a fucking clue what he was on about.

He was pacing back and forwards, saying again and again how I couldn't touch him, he was winding himself up….he was starting to breathe a bit faster and his tone was getting more aggressive. I was still in my thinkers stance and kept my eye on him as he prowled back and forth….then he gave me the signal.

He stepped forward and raised his right hand, I shot my left hand out in a short jab, right on his chin, not hard but hard enough. He looked a little shocked and rocked then took a step back.

"That's assault…..he assaulted me!" he began shouting, two police men were nearby so he went and had a moan to him. They were two regular officers who patrolled that area, and knew the kind of shit we had to put up with.

They could see he was a knob, and they told him to move on before he got arrested for drunk and disorderly....the dickhead then started demanding their badge numbers as he was going to complain they weren't doing their jobs etc.

After twenty minutes or so I had to walk around to the front door for something, as I'm walking around the corner I hear a voice shouting "That's him...that's the cunt!"....it was my mate from earlier, he now had his coat on (he wasn't lying after all) and was standing with two of his pals, who looked at me apologetically.

I grinned and shook my head, carrying on to the front door.

After a couple of minutes I turned to go back round to the back door. As I approached the corner again his two pals were still standing, and he pushed them apart as I got closer.

"Cunt, cunt, cunt" he was shouting, and pointing each time he said it. I had to walk right up to them to pass, he was still shouting "Cunt" as I got within punching range, and I threw a straight right into his face, knocking him onto his arse.

For some reason he looked shocked again. Did this guy really think he could behave like that and nobody would do anything to him?

I stood over him, my right hand pulled back, cocked and ready to punch him again.

"I'm a cunt am I?" I said through clenched teeth... "Next time I'll fucking hit you more than once....now fuck off"....I stood back and looked at his pals... "Take him away will ya...before he gets a fucking good hiding"

They picked him up and starting walking him away, a couple of times he tried to wriggle out of their grip and come back, but they kept hold of him. At one point one of them gave him a clip around the ear, telling him to stop being a dickhead, or they would let him go and get filled in.

Every now and again when I was on the back door of The Den I would go for a wander downstairs, you could go down one staircase to the nightclub underneath, have a wander around, and then go back up a spiral staircase to the bar upstairs.

I'd been for a wander one night and came to the bottom of the spiral staircase, where one of the younger door lads, Pete (not his real name) was dealing with a customer. Pete was quite a decent size, and the customer was bigger again. They were having a discussion, and I could hear that Pete was trying to get him to walk up the stairs and leave, the customer was leaning against the wall, being quite casual and arrogant….I got the impression he was having a bit of a show off to his girlfriend and didn't intend going anywhere.

I stood back and watched for a little while, ready to step in if Pete needed a hand, I was trying to catch the customers eye…if he could see there were two of us he may decide just to go, but by now he was giving Pete the tough guy stare, showing his girlfriend how hard he was, I also noticed he was now holding his bottle of lager by the neck, as opposed to the body of the bottle.

Pete's "conflict management" skills weren't working, with some people they never will. Some people will stand and debate and argue with a doorman for ages, these tend to either be the more well educated people, who try to embarrass door supervisors by arguing using long, convoluted sentences because they think we are all stupid thugs, or those who aren't interested in talking or reasoning, and what brief discussion you have with these people will usually end in a violent confrontation, as you can't reason with these people, they only respond to violence.

Pete's patience was starting to wear thin with this guy, and the longer the debate was going on, the more smug the guy was getting thinking he was making Pete look stupid. Eventually Pete told him he had to leave, and put his hand on the guys elbow to prompt him to move.

"Get your fucking hands off me" the guy shouts. He leaned forward off the wall and as he did so he brought his hand down against the wall, smashing the bottle, and pushed Pete back with his other hand.

I leapt forward grabbing his wrist with one hand, and grabbing him by the throat with the other, I wasn't going to fuck about with this guy; I wanted him out of action as quickly as possible, and to do that I wanted him unconscious. I pushed him back against the wall and he dropped the remains of the bottle, I was reaching up (as he was taller than me) with my right hand trying to choke him, and we were starting to slide along the wall as he got weaker. I knew he had dropped the bottle so I went for the choke with both hands. His girlfriend was screaming behind us and Pete was tied up with her. Once I got both hands on he started to go, he was trying to punch and grab me, but I had my head tucked in and my shoulders hunched up so he couldn't do anything effective.

After a bit of a struggle he passed out and slid down the wall, unconscious. I released my grip and lay him on his side in the recovery position....his girlfriend was going berserk, so I told Pete to let her go.

"Listen"...I said, as he crouched down beside her boyfriends head, crying, "I don't care what happened before....I'm a first aider, and I'm gonna look after him now".

She settled down a bit and told me him name; the usual nurses and army medics who were out on the drink appeared but Pete kept them back.

I couldn't get a response from the guy initially; but he was breathing, so I thought we would give him a little time to come round....I have done this before and people have lay there and started snoring!

His breathing was nice and steady, and I was leaning over him checking he wasn't bleeding from anywhere when I heard glass smashing and felt glass and splashes on the back of my head.

People were throwing bottles at us from the top of the stairs, a couple smashed against the wall above me, and some on the tiled floor next to where I was kneeling....Pete called it in and a scuffle ensued upstairs as they were sorted out by door staff.

The guy started to come round, and the three of us were covered in broken glass and beer....I was braced for him to kick off again but he didn't. He was a bit groggy but between us we managed to get him upstairs and to the back door. We got him outside in the fresh air and he was as good as gold, he shook my hand and thanked me for looking after him. He then asked if I could go and get the doorman who had choked him out, so he could apologize for being a dickhead....he didn't realize it was me who had done it, and then looked after him....his girlfriend and I looked at each other, I winked at her and shook my head, smiling.

"Come on....Let's get you home" she said to him, ushering him away from the door. I don't know how far or where they were going, but they wouldn't have got a taxi as he was a right mess....his clothes were soaking wet, his shirt was hanging out and he was stinking of lager!

Pete and I looked at each other, had a big sigh and a little chuckle to ourselves, then Pete returned back downstairs and I stood in the back door, picking the little bits of broken glass off my jacket.

The Final Chapter?

I have always been ambitious, in everything I have ever done. Once I had finished my apprenticeship I wanted to be self employed; when I was on the "career ladder" I wanted to be a Director….I wanted to be in charge.

It was the same on the doors, I wanted to be in charge, I wanted to be the Head Doorman. It used to frustrate me when I was working in a club and the Head Doorman was in the role not because of their experience or ability, but because of their size or because the club management like them.

I have worked in a couple of venues where the Head Doorman wasn't up to the job, was known to run from trouble or to just stand back and let others sort the shit out, but was there purely to keep the venue managers happy and therefore keep the contract.

Once or twice I was almost appointed the position, but the people I was working for were overruled by the venue manager and the role given to someone else.

I was however, asked to work at a large nightclub in Newcastle as the internal head doorman. The team inside the venue was a bit young and inexperienced, and the mind set was that maybe putting an older guy, who was also a trainer in charge of them might help them develop and calm them down a bit…..and then very soon after, I was offered the position of Head Doorman of a new nightclub in a town outside of Newcastle.

I had achieved my goals and aspirations.
The thing is though, even though I had achieved my goals,
I did not feel euphoric, I didn't even feel happy....I felt as if
now there is no further to go... "be careful what you wish
for"...they say....once you get to where you want be, where
do you go from there?

Over the years I had worked at a club called LQ a number
of times. In the past it was also called Liquid, Ikon, Ritzy,
Studio, Tiffany's and The Oxford. It has been around for
years, however at time of writing plans have been
submitted to convert the club into student
accommodation.
The first time I worked there the venue was still known as
Liquid, and I used to go along after working at other
venues to help disperse the crowd as they left the club at
the end of the night.
It used to regularly host student nights called "Carnage";
which were basically a pub crawl around the city centre
bars, and ending in the nightclub. The theme for this
particular carnage event was doctors and nurses, so all of
the girls donned sexy underwear and skimpy nurses outfits,
and all the guys wore white doctors coats over their
clothes. I had never the seen the club as busy as it was that
night; I was standing upstairs in the VIP area with the
internal head doorman, and we were looking down
through the glass wall onto the dance floor.
The dance floor was a sea of white, it was so busy you
couldn't see the floor, just a mass of white outfits....then it
kicked off.....and it was like a pebble being dropped into a
pond and the ripples spreading outwards.
The trouble started in the middle of the dance floor, and as
they jostled and scrapped more people joined in. it was
that busy the door staff couldn't get through the crowd to
take control. The guy upstairs with me called it in and went
running downstairs, but at the bottom of the stairs he hit a

mass of bodies, which he then had to force his way through to get to the dance floor…which was about fifteen metres away from the bottom of the stairs.

To be fair there was nothing the door staff could do at that point; somebody signaled to the DJ and the music was turned off, then all the lights were turned on. An announcement was made that if the fighting carried on the club would close, this seemed to do the trick and people in the crowd started to stop the fighting. The door staff then went around picking the trouble makers out and ejecting them.

This was around the time that the club was changing owners, and changed from Liquid to LQ, we knew it had been / was being bought out by an Asian guy, but that's all we knew. To get in the VIP suite you had to be wearing a wristband, so I was to ensure that anybody trying to get in had their wristband on, and anybody without one didn't get in.

Three Asian guys came up to the door and tried to walk past me.

"Got your wristbands lads?" I asked.

The one in front smiled "We don't need them" he said.

"Really….well I say you do" I replied, smiling.

"Go and see your head doorman downstairs…he will tell you it's ok" was his reply.

"Tell you what"….I said, closing the door behind me, "You go and get him, bring him back here, and then he can tell me it's ok….ok?"

He didn't look amused, and was getting a little pissed off… "Do you know who I am?" he asked

I took a deep breath and thought "Fucking hell….not another one"…..

"No mate…I don't know who you are, do you have any I,D?….it'll probably tell you on that who you are…or ask one of your mates, they probably know"….I was on a roll now and looked at one of his pals "Do you know who he

is?" I asked…. "Can you tell him cos he doesn't know"
"I'm the new owner" he said, and told me his name…with a very straight, solemn face…. Then the manager came through the door behind and ushered them in.
"Fucking Bastard" I thought to myself… I felt a right idiot.
He walked past and smirked, as did his two pals, to be fair he had some wristbands brought up later on; and made a joke of it for the rest of the night.

The club would hold regular "Ikon" nights. On these nights DJ's and artists from the era when the club was known as Ikon would come and perform, playing the same music as they would have played back in the day…. It was Boxing day 2013, and the Ikon event was on.
The guy who would normally act as Internal Head hadn't turned in, so I was asked to do it….
It wasn't going too bad until we got a shout to bar one, it was a code red so we all attended, anyway it was a bit of a cluster fuck with everyone restraining people and trying to find out what happened….but one chunky lad in particular (who turned out to be the instigator) was being a particular pain in the arse. He had sucker punched a guy in the back of the head who was dancing beside him, and then, much to his surprise, the guy had turned around and punched him back, cutting his mouth.
One of the guys had restrained him (the instigator), and I went across to give him a hand and get him out, he was protesting that he hadn't started it etc, and as he spoke he was spitting blood in our faces and onto our shirts….nice.
We convinced him to walk down to the front door; and as him and his pal were walking along behind another DS, with me behind him, he was giving it the big un to his pal…..shadow boxing, saying how he was gonna knock us all out etc.
We get him outside and he walks around to other side of the barriers, which are about waist height, and the

doorman (P) who initially restrained him inside had come out, and they start chatting over the barrier. The chat quickly turns into a heated debated about P taking liberties etc, and I could tell it was gonna go off at some point....I stood just to the side of P, slightly on an angle, facing the arsehole, with my right hand poised by my side....I had a clear shot of his chin should he kick off.

Then his brother comes out the club and squares up to P, now we had two of them on one side of the railing, but one on the same side as us, his brother was taller than both me and P, and quickly made me more convinced that this was gonna go bad....and quick.

He had backed into the corner of the barriers, and was in P's face; adamant that P had smacked his brother inside. I was trying to keep eyes on all three of them when P kicked the barriers open and pushed the brother through the opening....the arsehole who had been thrown out raised his fist and looked towards P.....here we go I thought to myself!

I launched myself at him and drove a straight punch into his already bloodied face, to be fair I can't remember the next couple of seconds....which is scary, it means I wasn't in control. I must have took a couple of shots as well....as I ended up with a cut lip, cut head, and bruising to my ear.

The next thing I remember I have him bent in front of me, facing down. I have hold of his hair and I am driving uppercut after uppercut into his face....by rights I should have dragged him down and restrained him, or knocked him to the ground and restrained him....but I wanted to keep hitting him...I was holding him up so I could hurt him more....P then grabbed him and took him to the ground, restraining him.

I turned and faced his brother, who was stepping towards me, he was bleeding from the nose and mouth as the other lads had already gave him the good news and put him on his arse....as he stepped forward, I raised my hands up in a classic boxers stance, and hunched up....planning which shot I was gonna throw first. I was ready for him, and even called him on, encouraging him to have a go; but he backed off. He had been clipped and put on his arse once, and I don't think he fancied ending up like his brother....pinned to the floor....bleeding.

The police then turned up and they both got arrested. The one who wasn't pinned down made a run for it, after threatening to come back and do us all in one by one. A couple of doormen and police gave chase and caught him. The police came back and asked if we wanted to press charges, which we didn't. In my opinion that's not how it works, and I detest people who start fights in bars or with doormen, and then when they get beat go crying to the police that they have been assaulted. If you can't accept it if you get beat; then don't cause bother in the first place....to be fair though, on this occasion I was shitting myself in case he pressed charges, as I would be struggling to claim self defense this time!

Normally if I need to wind down after work I will get food on the way home, and sit somewhere in the car and eat it.

I always park away from the venue where I'm working, and when I get back to the car I check around the wheels for bottles, broken glass, or anything else which could damage the car and stop me driving away.

I have a number of different routes I take home, and if I am getting food on the way home there are a number of different places I go for it. On the drive home I am always conscious of being followed. I have known a couple of guys be followed home from work before, if I think somebody is following me then I adopt various counter surveillance methods, I will go around roundabouts a couple of times before turning off, indicate one way and turn another, turn sharply without indicating, or just keep driving away from home.

Some people may think I am being silly and paranoid, and you do treat all the threats of comebacks with the contempt that they deserve, but you never know, and you can never be too careful.

I woke the next morning around eleven and assessed the damage from the night before. The cut on my top lip had been bleeding through the night and had scabbed over, there was another on the top of my head. My neck was stiff and aching, the insides of both my forearms were bruised, and my right hand was pretty sore. I knew at the time that my lip was cut, but didn't feel anything else anywhere on my body at the time. The adrenaline release stops you feeling pain and also causes some muscles to cramp up during the incident, which is probably why I had a stiff neck.

There was no time for moaning and seeking sympathy though, I had a two o clock start that afternoon at the club. We were looking after a works Christmas party for a large business based on a local trading estate. Thankfully the event finished without incident, and I was homeward bound at eight o clock

A couple of days after the works party; on a Sunday, three of us worked on an "Iranian Party". These were held in the club every year, and singers or bands who were popular with the Iranian / Persian community were brought in. It was quite a busy night; with people turning up with kids in buggies and young children. All of the women were attractive, one of the lads working with me fell in love many times that night.

While we were standing around chatting about Boxing day and other experiences, I was thinking "How much longer do I want to do this for?" It wasn't a reflection on the guys I was working with, it had been bubbling around inside me for a while.

I was also finding I was going in harder for physical confrontations, if I couldn't resolve a situation verbally and it went hands on, I would try to end it as quickly and as effectively as possible, I would go from being rational to irrational in a tenth of a second. I had no interest in rolling around on the floor fighting and trying to restrain people....was I becoming as bad as the people I was fighting against?

I didn't miss it any more when I wasn't working, I could take it or leave it.

I took New Years Eve off, the first one in eight years, and I had pretty much decided by then that I would have a bit of a break..

Hopefully I can carry on with my training business. I am qualified to deliver training in Door Supervision, Security Guarding, Physical Intervention, Conflict Management, CCTV and First Aid. I am also waiting for my license to teach close protection.

I enjoy delivering the training, especially door supervision. It's easy, I can talk all day about something I enjoy doing, and there are probably not many aspects of the job I haven't experienced.

At time of writing I have worked in twenty seven venues over twenty four years, as well as some private functions.

I have worked in dockers bars, strip clubs, rock clubs, gay bars, and some of the biggest nightclubs in a major city centre.

I have been punched, kicked, bitten, stamped on, attacked with bottles, glasses, high heels and handbags.

Over the last few years I have "packed in" a number of times, then somebody will contact me to help out and do a cover shift, then I am sucked back in again. That's what Donna says every time I tell her I am packing in "We'll see.......Just wait until someone rings you up for a shift".

Guess I better not throw my boots and earpieces out just yet!

ABOUT THE AUTHOR

Neil Sarin is 43 and lives with his wife and three sons in the North East of England. He also has two daughters and a granddaughter.

He has over twenty years of experience working on pub and nightclub doors, in and around Newcastle Upon Tyne; he has been there, done that, and got the blood stained tee shirt.

As well as working the doors; he is also a qualified security industry trainer, and first aid instructor.

For training or advice, Neil can be contacted on:
neil.sarin@blueyonder.co.uk
Or via the "Big Lads and Handbags" facebook page.

.

25911440R00064

Made in the USA
Charleston, SC
19 January 2014